N scale
MODEL RAILROAD
track plans

MODEL RAILROAD HANDBOOK NO. 7

KALMBACH BOOKS

First printing, 1969. Second printing, 1970. Third printing, 1971. Fourth printing, 1973. Fifth printing, 1974. Sixth printing, 1976. Seventh printing, 1979. Eighth printing, 1982. Ninth printing, 1984. Tenth printing, 1986. Eleventh printing, 1988. Twelfth printing, 1989. Thirteenth printing, 1991.

Gauge is the distance between rails measured from inside to inside. N gauge is equal to 9 millimeters (.355″).

N scale track information

Scale and gauge

Scale is the relationship between the model and the item being modeled (called the prototype). This relationship is 1:160 for N scale.

Gauge is the distance between the rails measured from inside to inside. Standard prototype rail gauge is 4′-8½″. N gauge is equal to 4′-8½″ divided by 160, or 9 millimeters. Millimeters are usually used instead of inches because the pioneering work in N scale was done in Europe, where the meter instead of the foot is the standard unit of length. (The track gauge in inches is .355″.)

To get a better "feel" for N scale, let's compare an N scale boxcar with the prototype. It would take 160 N scale boxcars laid end to end to equal the prototype length. Likewise, it would take 160 models placed side by side to equal the prototype width, and a stack 160 high to equal the height. To fill the same space (volume) a real boxcar does, it would take a solid stack of N scale models 160 long by 160 wide by 160 high. Such a stack would contain 4,096,000 N scale boxcars.

N gauge sectional track

Train sets usually include pieces of track which when joined together form an oval or other simple track plan. This type of track is called sec-

tional track. This is the easiest track to work with and is usually considered ideal for beginners. The advantage of sectional track is that it can be assembled easily without any cutting or other handwork. A disadvantage is that track plans using sectional track must be designed around fixed-radius curves. However, there are many track configurations possible with sectional track, as this book illustrates.

Flexible track is a special type of sectional track. Different manufacturers offer slightly different lengths but they're all around 3 feet. This track can easily be formed into any type of curve. There are spaces in the plastic supporting strips under the rails which make it flexible. Using flexible track you can achieve a more realistic layout because you're not tied to fixed-radius curves. A disadvantage, for the beginner, is that some rail cutting is required. When a section of flexible track is curved, the rail ends come out uneven, and the longer one must be cut back with a razor saw. Also, some of the 3-foot lengths will have to be cut into shorter pieces for some trackwork.

Before you decide which type of sectional track to buy — fixed radius or flexible — look at both and ask your hobby shop man for his opinion.

The plans presented in this book are for fixed-radius sectional track. However, you can construct all of the railroads with flexible track. Also, using the dimensions given you can roughly calculate the number of pieces of flexible track needed.

Interchangeability

N gauge sectional track currently available uses two different methods of joining sections together. This af-

Train sets usually include pieces of sectional track which when joined together form an oval.

Standard prototype rail gauge in the United States is 4'-8½" measured from inside to inside.

It would take 4,096,000 N scale boxcars to fill a prototype boxcar.

fects interchangeability of different makes. The usual method uses in-line rail joiners (fishplates), while the other uses staggered rail joiners. If necessary the two types can be joined to each other by cutting one rail of one type to match the other type.

Each manufacturer of N gauge sectional track offers different radii of curves, different types of switches, and different lengths of straight track. This lack of standardization can be an advantage when you combine different makes of track on your layout, making more arrangements possible. Remember to stay with the same type of rail joiners, however, using either all in-line or all staggered.

Radius and degrees

A label such as "9¾" r, 30-degree section" is a common way curved pieces of sectional track are identified. The radius, r, is measured from the center of a circle of track to a point midway between the rails. The number of degrees per section indicates how many pieces are required to form a complete circle. For instance, it takes 12 30-degree pieces to form a complete circle (360 degrees).

Laying sectional track

Homasote board is a very good material to use for your railroad tabletop. It is a type of wall board sold in most lumberyards. It is less

expensive than plywood and it also has sound deadening properties. Homasote is the recommended material to use with the "hard shell" scenery method which you will probably want to try later.*

It is advisable to take the time to draw the track plan on the mounting board. Locate holes for electrical connections and openings which may have to be cut for switch machines.

If you're improvising a plan, be sure to consider the minimum track spacing for two trains to pass on any parallel tracks without sideswiping.

*This method of building scenery is described in Bill McClanahan's book SCENERY FOR MODEL RAILROADS.

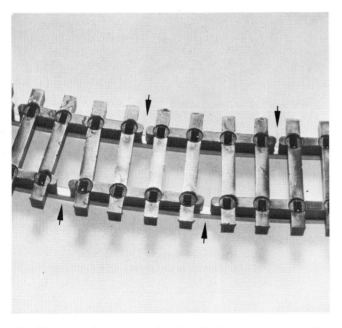

Flexible track has spaces in the plastic supporting strips under the rails which make it flexible.

Most makes of N gauge track use in-line rail joiners. Some use staggered rail joiners.

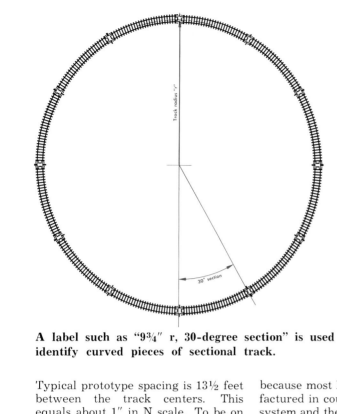

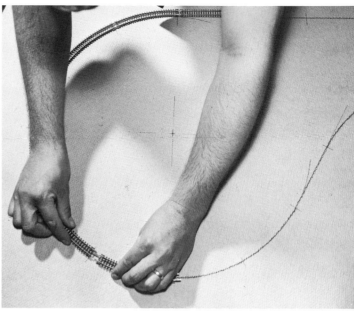

A label such as "9¾″ r, 30-degree section" is used to identify curved pieces of sectional track.

Join all the track sections together on the mounting board and see how the track fits the penciled diagram.

Typical prototype spacing is 13½ feet between the track centers. This equals about 1″ in N scale. To be on the safe side, use a center-to-center track spacing of 1¼″ to 1½″.

Join all the track sections together on the mounting board. There are mounting holes in the center of the end ties of each section and usually in one tie near the center. Drive in several nails at strategic locations to see how the assembled track fits the penciled diagram. If you use the dimensions given by the manufacturer the track may not fit the plan exactly, because most N gauge track is manufactured in countries using the metric system and the conversion from millimeters to inches doesn't work out exactly. Shift the track position to distribute any error evenly.

The track can be mounted permanently with nails or a combination of glue and nails. The small nails required can be pressed into the Homasote board with a pair of long-nose pliers. If you aren't satisfied with the results obtained by placing a nail in each available hole you can drill additional holes with a pin vise. Another way to mount the track to the board permanently is to lay a strip of white glue down the center of the ties. White glue takes some time to dry, so you can do the final positioning and then place books or other suitable weights on top of the track until the glue dries. It's best to let it dry overnight.

Track mounted with white glue can later be taken up by placing hot damp towels on the track to soften the glue.

When mounting your track take extra time to avoid kinks at the rail joints. Kinks cause derailments.

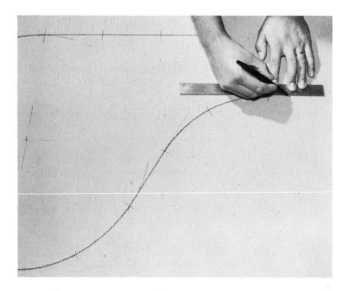

Take the time to draw the track plan on the mounting board. It will make track mounting easier.

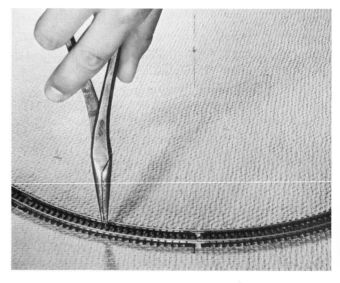

The small nails required for mounting can be pressed into the Homasote board with a pair of long-nose pliers.

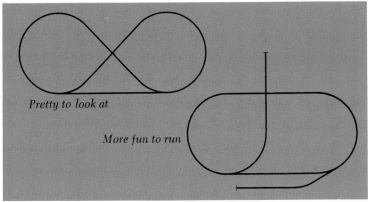

Pretty to look at

More fun to run

Station

Prototypical track planning

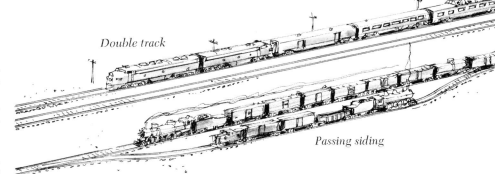

Double track

Passing siding

SOME track plans look like pretty designs, but they may not be as much fun for running trains as a plan that is more like a real railroad track plan. Also, if you think about your railroad a little bit, you can make a better plan with fewer switches and other expensive pieces of track.

There's a secret to making a plan that's more fun. Make it as much like a real railroad as you can.

Oh, you can't do all the things a real railroad does — maybe hardly any of them — but what you can do will be better than just setting your railroad up like a Christmas toy. You know, real model railroading is a hobby for every week in the year, and it can be even more fun than some movie and television shows. With a model railroad you don't just watch; you run things yourself.

What does a real railroad track plan have that you can build too?

A real railroad has stations for loading passengers and some kinds of freight. It also has spur tracks and sidings where freight cars that take long-

er to load or empty can be put. Without separate tracks, these cars would block the main line.

The railroad has to have a main line so trains can go from one part of the country to another. If there are many trains, the railroad will have two or even more tracks; this happens near cities like New York and Chicago. Farther away from big cities most railroads have only one main track, but then they have a sidetrack every few miles or so where slow trains can get out of the way of fast trains and where trains coming from both directions can make a "meet."

On a model railroad a double track may seem glamorous; it's fun to watch trains fly by each other on double track, too. But there's another kind of fun you should try with single track, and that is to make meets and passes in the sidetracks.

What to do with switches

When you get a pair of switches you can use them to make a passing siding, or you can build a cutoff from one part of the main line to another. The cutoff gives operating variety because the train dosen't always have to go the same way.

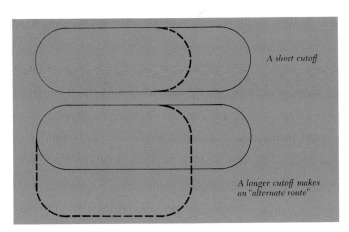

A short cutoff

A longer cutoff makes an "alternate route"

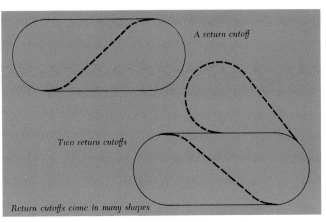

A return cutoff

Two return cutoffs

Return cutoffs come in many shapes

5

PLANS FOR LARGE SPACES

You'll often need short "fitters" to make a crossing join with other tracks

All the plans in this book can be fitted into larger spaces by adding more straight track and/or using larger-radius track. Most manufacturers of N gauge track offer track with radii of from 16″ to 19″ for large sweeping curves. If you can, add some of the track diagonally in the corners for variety.

Another good idea is to keep the track away from the edges of your space. This leaves room for more scenery; also, if the railroad is on a table you won't have trains falling to the floor.

If you lay the railroad on a bias, it will look better than if you lay it parallel to the table. The wedges of space create more scenic variety than a uniformly shaped space.

Extra pieces of fitter track

It may seem like a nuisance to provide yourself with some short lengths of straight track, but these fitters will be a lifesaver many times. You can make hundreds more track arrangements in the same space using fitters. The reason is that you don't have to have the regular track come out just right in closing a loop.

Fitters are especially needed when you use a crossing, and they help in plans that require many switches. On the other hand, you can often build a railroad without fitters by bending the track a little or by interchanging the position of a straight track with a curve near it.

Mainline running

While switching is usually the most fun on a small railroad, you'll want to have some mainline track for sure. If space is small, some kind of an oval or figure eight is about the best you can do. These types of plans allow you to run the train over and over the same track for a long time.

Once in a while you should try a "point-to-point" railroad. Using what

Spurs and stub sidings give you the most effective use of switches

With two switches you can also make a "return cutoff"; this not only adds variety of route, but it also turns the train the other way for still another kind of variety. It's best to use four switches and make two return cutoffs instead of one. This lets you turn a train from clockwise to counterclockwise running and then reverse it again without backing up.

Cutoffs and sidings usually require two switches for each. But if you build stub sidings and spur tracks to serve several factories and other kinds of industries, you'll get the most use out of your switches because it takes only one instead of two switches to join a spur to the main line. Usually it's better to save about half of your switches for this kind of track. Since

you can put spurs almost anywhere along the main line, you can change them around every day or so for variety.

Crossings add interest

Crossings are used at a place where one track must cross another and a bridge isn't practical.

Don't call a crossing a "crossover," because it isn't a crossover. A *crossing* is where two tracks cross each

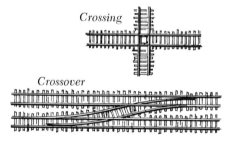

Crossing

Crossover

other. A *crossover* is made by locating two switches so that a train is able to slip from one track over to the next. Notice the crossing and crossover in the sketch above.

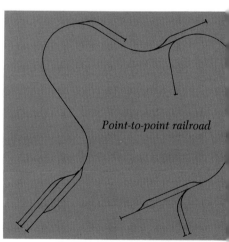

Point-to-point railroad

Main line

switches you have, build a small yard at each end of a long winding main line. You can save switches by building a "return loop" at one end and pretending the train is at a different place when it gets back. This makes a "point-to-loop" type of plan.

You won't need passing tracks along the main line unless you plan to run more than one train at the same time, but it will make things more interesting if you add a factory spur here and there.

Way freight operation

A way freight is a train that stops at every spur and freight siding to deliver cars and pick up other cars. This kind of local train is a great deal of fun to operate and it will present you with puzzles to solve, too. For instance, how do you push car C into the sidetrack in this plan:

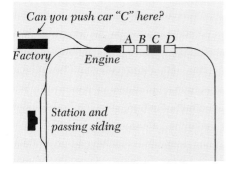

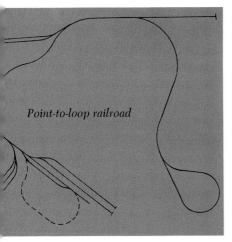

Point-to-loop railroad

Available N scale trackage

BRAND	STRAIGHT	CURVED	CROSSINGS	SWITCHES	OTHER
AHM (Associated Hobby Manufacturers)	3¾" — Code 80 rail — See note 1	7" r 30° 9" r 21° 9" r 24° 9" r 45°	RH 24° LH 24°	RH & LH Remote 9" r 24°	
ATLAS	5" 2½" 1¼" — Code 80 rail — See note 1	9¾" r 30° 9¾" r 15° 11" r 30° 11" r 15° 19" r 15°	15° 90°	RH & LH manual & remote 19" r 15°	RH & LH #6 remote switches --- 30" sections of flexible track
ARNOLD RAPIDO [1]	9" 4½" 2¼" — Code 80 rail — See note 1	8" r 90° 8" r 45° 8" r 15° 9" r 45° 9" r 15° 17" r 30° 17" r 15°	Note 2	RH & LH manual & remote 17" r 15° --- Manual & remote double slip switches	Telescoping track sections --- 27" sections of flexible track
BACHMANN	9" 4½" 2¼" 1⅛" — Code 80 rail — See note 1	8" r 90° 8" r 45° 8" r 22½° 8" r 15° 8" r 11¼° 9" r 45° 9" r 15°	15° 90°	RH & LH manual & remote	9" & 4½" straight terminal sections
CON-COR [2]	6⅛" 2" — Code 80 rail — See note 1	12½" r 30° 12½" r 10°	Note 2	Note 2	32" sections of flexible track
KEMTRON	Note 2 — Code 70 & code 40 rail — See note 1	Note 2	Note 2	Note 2	32" sections of flexible track
MINITRIX [3]	12" 4⅛" 3" 2⅛" 2" 1⅛" — Code 80 rail — See note 1	7½" r 30° 7½" r 24° 7½" r 6° 9" r 30° 9" r 24° 9" r 6°	30°	RH & LH manual & remote 7½" r 24° + 6° --- Remote double slip switch	7½" r 30° terminal section
PECO	Note 2 Code 80 rail — See note 1	Note 2	8° 25°	RH & LH manual & remote 36" r, 30" r, 18" r, & 9" r	36" sections of flexible track

1 — Also used by Revell   2 — Also used by Model Rectifier Corporation

Note 1 — Rail height is designated by a code number. This number is equal to the height of the rail in thousandths of an inch. In N scale the rail is not strictly standard, but the rail height will be within several thousandths of the code number listed.

Note 2 — The table lists what is offered by major brands of N scale track at the time of publication. Because N scale is relatively new, additional track components will undoubtedly be offered in the coming years. Your hobby shop man can keep you informed on new developments in N scale.

The brands of track shown in the following plans are representative of the many fine lines of N scale track available today. We have included specific information for as many brands of track as we feel is practical in one book of this type.

Railroads without switches

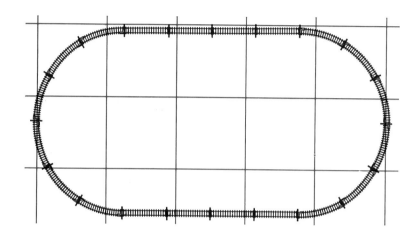

MOST train sets contain enough track to build an oval. Ovals, or "laps," can be made to fit any-size table. The shape of the lap can be varied somewhat by putting some straight pieces in the corners. Each time you add straight pieces of track to both sides of the plan, you make the plan longer. But if you put straight track in the corners, you make the plan both longer and wider.

When you add curves so that one side turns inward, you need a lot more space, but you get a much better effect for scenery.

If you plan to build your railroad along the walls of a basement or garage, the corner arrangement of these plans is good, but try to keep the track far enough from the wall so that you can get some scenery behind the track as well as in front of it.

The easiest way to handle two trains at the same time is by using a two-oval plan. Where tracks run parallel, arrange buildings and roads for a busy double-track effect.

PLAN 1 (AHM)

BRAND	STRAIGHT	CURVED	SIZE
AHM	8 - 3¾"	12 - 7"r 30°	16" x 32"
Arnold Rapido[1]	4 - 9"	8 - 8"r 45°	16" x 34"
Atlas	8 - 5"	12 - 9¾"r 30°	22" x 40"
Minitrix[2]	2 - 12" 2 - 4⅛"	12 - 7½"r 30°	16" x 32"

1 — Also sold by Revell
2 — Also sold by Aurora

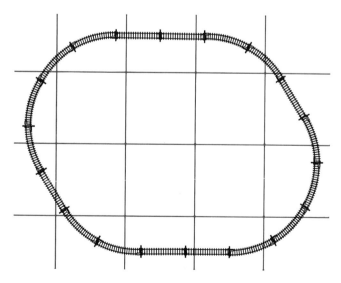

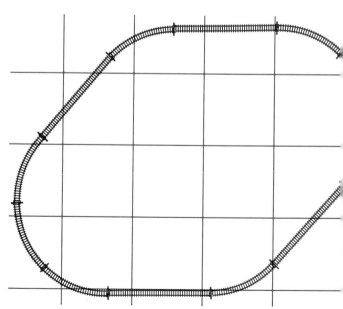

PLAN 2 (AHM)

BRAND	STRAIGHT	CURVED	SIZE
AHM	6 - 3¾"	12 - 7"r 30°	20" x 26"
Atlas	6 - 5"	12 - 9¾"r 30°	26" x 34"
Minitrix[1]	6 - 4⅛"	12 - 7½"r 30°	24" x 30"

1 — Also sold by Aurora

PLAN 3 (Arnold Rapido)

BRAND	STRAIGHT	CURVED	SIZE
Arnold Rapido[1]	4 - 9"	8 - 8"r 45°	24" x 32"

1 — Also sold by Revell

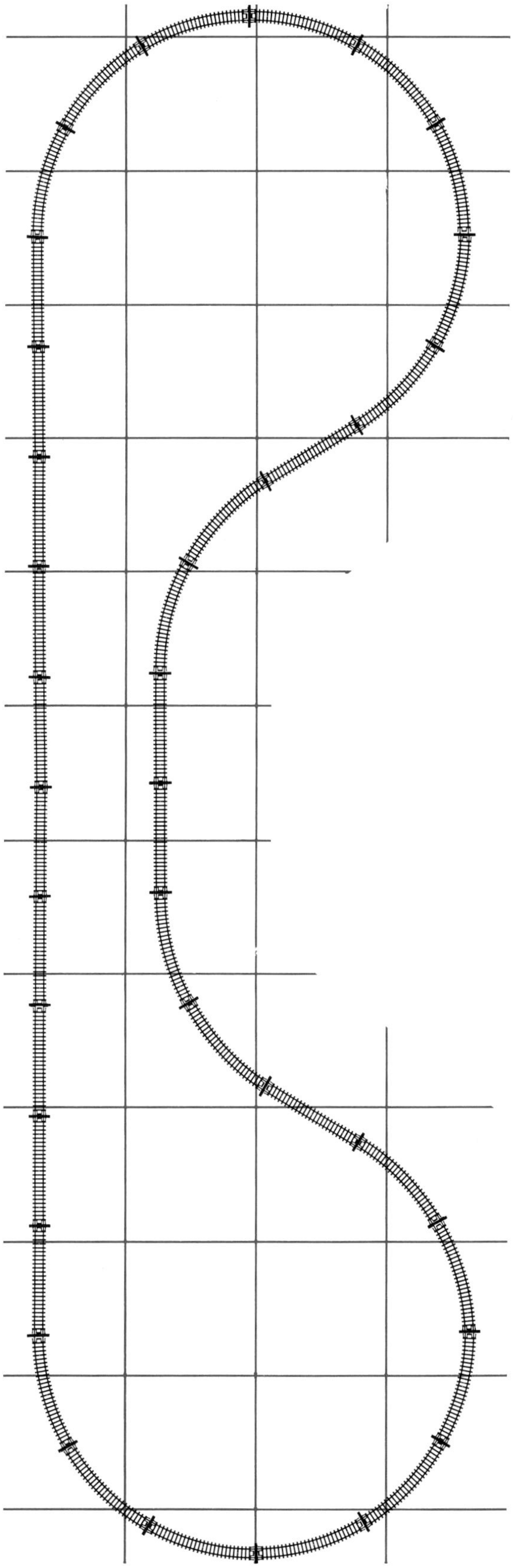

PLAN 4 (Atlas)

BRAND	STRAIGHT	CURVED	SIZE
AHM	15 - 3¾″	20 - 7″r 30°	16″ x 54″
Arnold Rapido[1]	8 - 9″	12 - 8″r 45°	16″ x 60″
Atlas	14 - 5″	20 - 9¾″r 30°	22″ x 70″

1 — Also sold by Revell

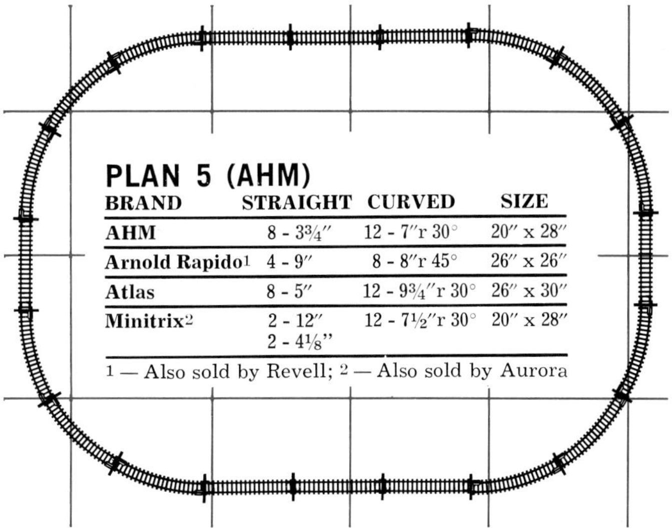

PLAN 5 (AHM)

BRAND	STRAIGHT	CURVED	SIZE
AHM	8 - 3¾″	12 - 7″r 30°	20″ x 28″
Arnold Rapido[1]	4 - 9″	8 - 8″r 45°	26″ x 26″
Atlas	8 - 5″	12 - 9¾″r 30°	26″ x 30″
Minitrix[2]	2 - 12″ 2 - 4⅛"	12 - 7½″r 30°	20″ x 28″

1 — Also sold by Revell; 2 — Also sold by Aurora

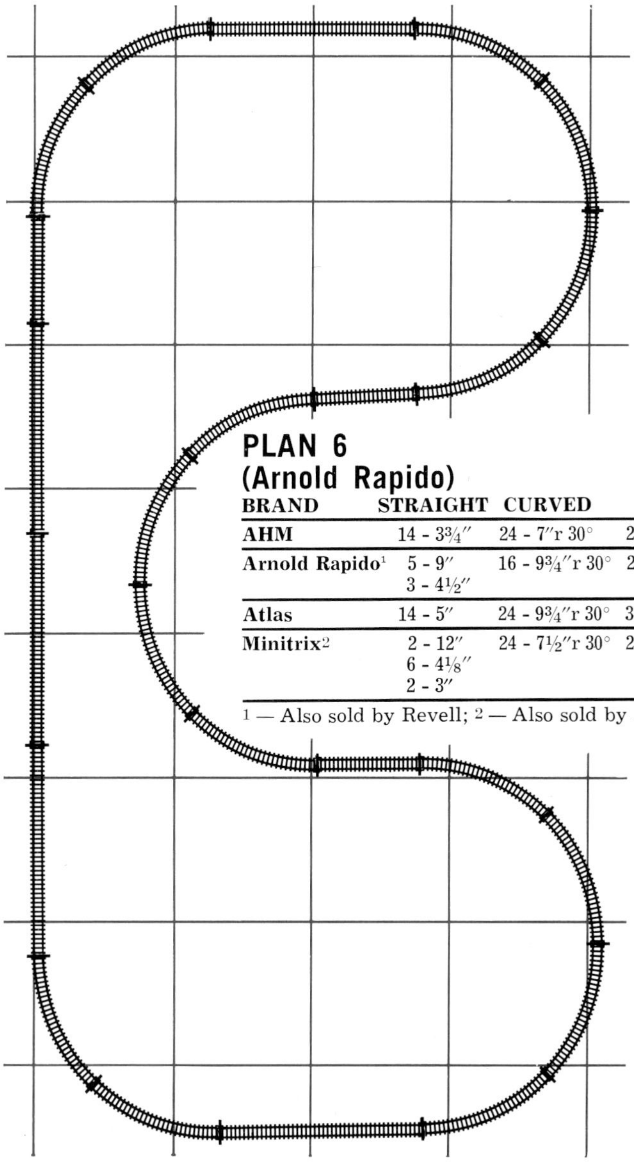

PLAN 6 (Arnold Rapido)

BRAND	STRAIGHT	CURVED	SIZE
AHM	14 - 3¾″	24 - 7″r 30°	24″ x 46″
Arnold Rapido[1]	5 - 9″ 3 - 4½″	16 - 9¾″r 30°	26″ x 48″
Atlas	14 - 5″	24 - 9¾″r 30°	30″ x 60″
Minitrix[2]	2 - 12″ 6 - 4⅛″ 2 - 3″	24 - 7½″r 30°	24″ x 46″

1 — Also sold by Revell; 2 — Also sold by Aurora

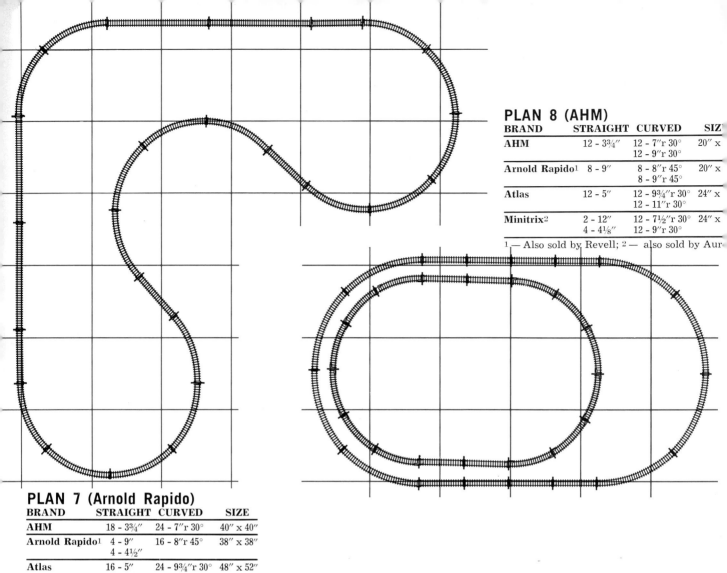

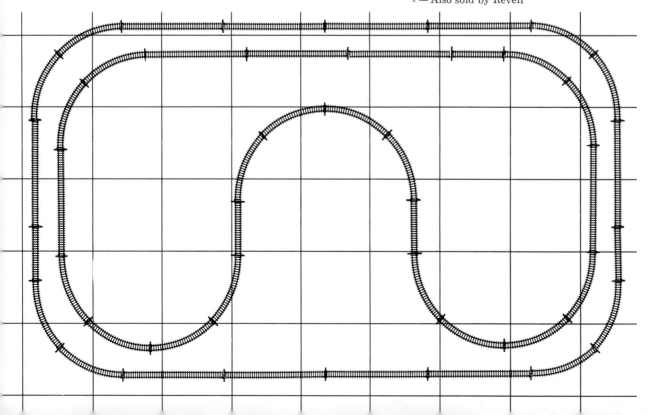

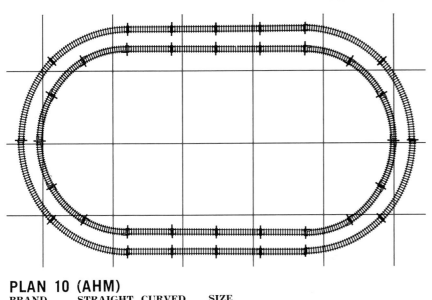

PLAN 10 (AHM)

BRAND	STRAIGHT	CURVED	SIZE
AHM	16 - 3¾"	12 - 7"r 30° 12 - 9"r 30°	20" x 34"
Arnold Rapido[1]	12 - 9"	8 - 8"r 45° 8 - 9"r 45°	20" x 46"
Atlas	16 - 5"	12 - 9¾"r 30° 12 - 11"r 30°	24" x 44"
Minitrix[2]	4 - 12" 4 - 4⅛"	12 - 7½"r 30° 12 - 9"r 30°	20" x 36"

1 — Also sold by Revell; 2 — also sold by Aurora.

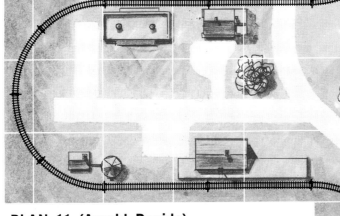

PLAN 11 (Arnold Rapido)

BRAND	STRAIGHT	CURVED	SIZE
AHM	24 - 3¾"	24 - 7"r 30°	46" x 62"
Arnold Rapido[1]	11 - 9" 1 - 4½"	16 - 8"r 45°	50" x 64"

1 — Also sold by Revell

The scenery suggestions shown on some of these plans are only a few of the many ways you can arrange roads, streams, hills, cliffs, buildings, and railroad accessories. You can pick the ideas from several plans and put them together on a different plan.

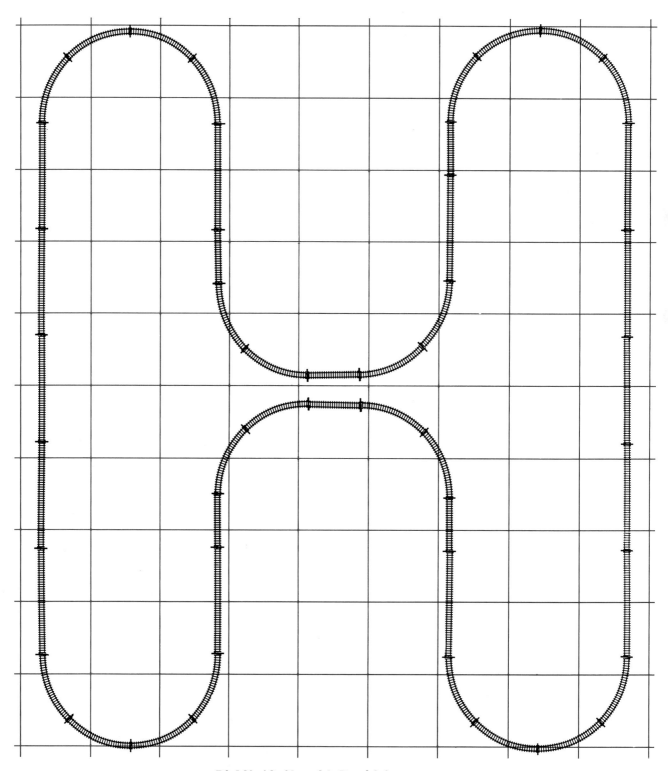

PLAN 12 (Arnold Rapido)

BRAND	STRAIGHT	CURVED	SIZE
Arnold Rapido[1]	14 - 9″ 6 - 4½″	24 - 8″r 45°	52″ x 60″

1 — Also sold by Revell

Railroads with crossings and overpasses

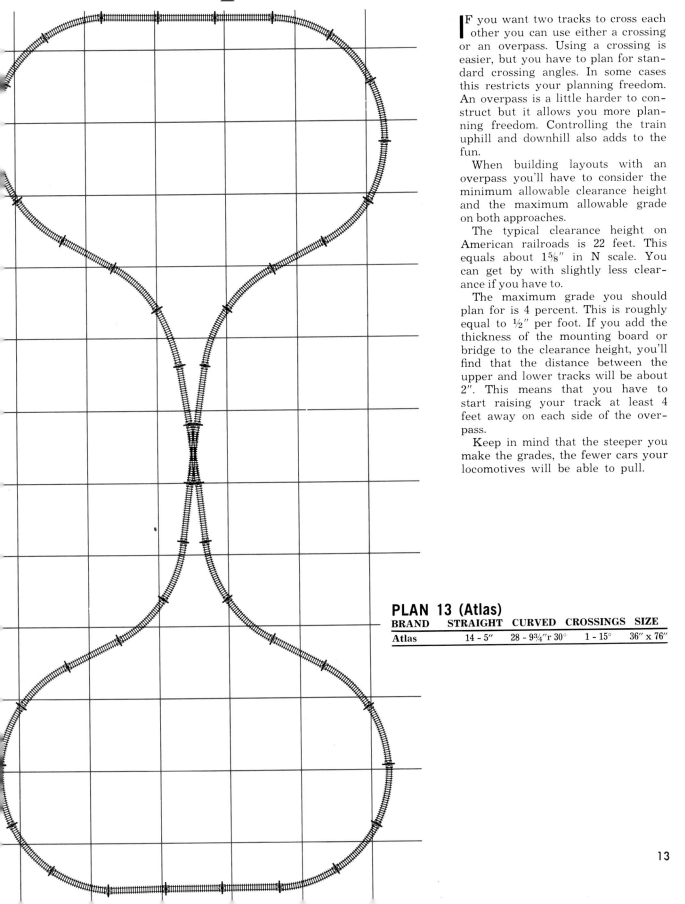

IF you want two tracks to cross each other you can use either a crossing or an overpass. Using a crossing is easier, but you have to plan for standard crossing angles. In some cases this restricts your planning freedom. An overpass is a little harder to construct but it allows you more planning freedom. Controlling the train uphill and downhill also adds to the fun.

When building layouts with an overpass you'll have to consider the minimum allowable clearance height and the maximum allowable grade on both approaches.

The typical clearance height on American railroads is 22 feet. This equals about $1\frac{5}{8}$″ in N scale. You can get by with slightly less clearance if you have to.

The maximum grade you should plan for is 4 percent. This is roughly equal to $\frac{1}{2}$″ per foot. If you add the thickness of the mounting board or bridge to the clearance height, you'll find that the distance between the upper and lower tracks will be about 2″. This means that you have to start raising your track at least 4 feet away on each side of the overpass.

Keep in mind that the steeper you make the grades, the fewer cars your locomotives will be able to pull.

PLAN 13 (Atlas)

BRAND	STRAIGHT	CURVED	CROSSINGS	SIZE
Atlas	14 - 5″	28 - 9¾″r 30°	1 - 15°	36″ x 76″

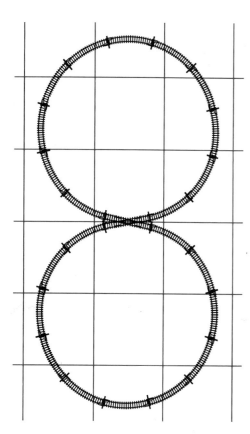

PLAN 14 (AHM)

BRAND	STRAIGHT	CURVED	CROSSINGS	SIZE
AHM	none	22 - 7"r 30°	1 - 24°	16" x 32"

PLAN 15 (Arnold Rapido)

BRAND	STRAIGHT	CURVED	SIZE
AHM	32 - 3¾"	24 - 7"r 30°	31" x 54"
Arnold Rapido[1]	16 - 9"	16 - 8"r 45°	34" x 60"
	2 - 4½"		
	2 - 2¼"		

[1] — Also sold by Revell

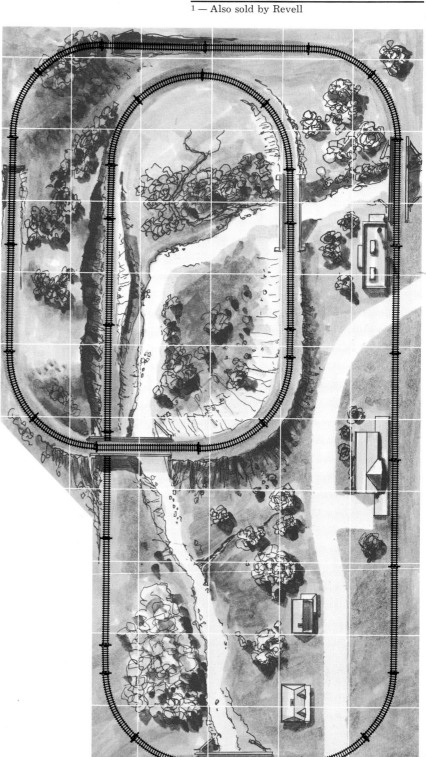

Short pieces of straight track may seem to be a nuisance, but they'll come in mighty handy many times. If fitters aren't available in the brand of track you're using, you can cut your own, using a razor saw. Razor saws are sold in most hobby shops and some hardware stores.

Railroads with one switch

FOR a minimum investment you can buy one switch and additional pieces of track to provide a spur or short branch line.

Some manufacturers of N scale track sell switches only in pairs (one left-hand switch and one right-hand switch), while others sell switches individually. If you're using a brand of track which sells switches only in pairs, then skip these plans and go on to those in the next section.

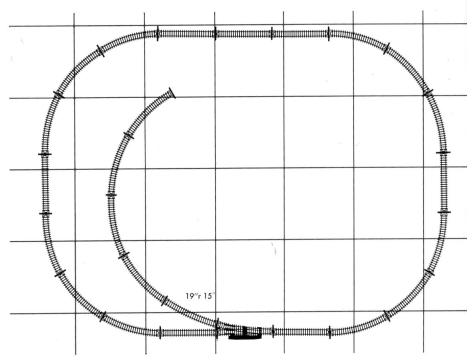

19"r 15°

PLAN 16 (Atlas)

BRAND	STRAIGHT	CURVED	SWITCHES	SIZE
AHM	7 - 3¾"	16 - 7"r 30"	1 RH	21" x 28"
Atlas	7 - 5"	16 - 9¾"r 30° 1 - 19"r 15°1	1 RH	27" x 36"
Minitrix2	7 - 4⅛"	16 - 7½"r 30°	1 RH	27" x 28"

1 — Atlas supplies one 19"r 15° piece with each switch
2 — Also sold by Aurora

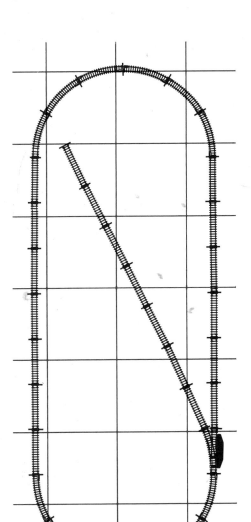

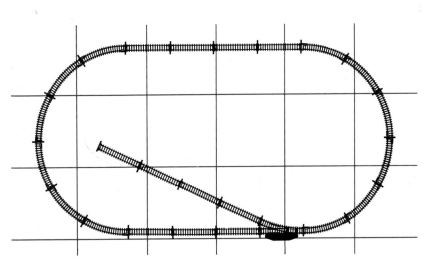

PLAN 17 (AHM)

BRAND	STRAIGHT	CURVED	SWITCHES	SIZE
AHM	20 - 3¾"	12 - 7"r 30°	1 LH	17" x 42"
Atlas	15 - 5"	12 - 9¾"r 30° 1 - 19"r 15°1	1 LH	22" x 50"
Minitrix2	3 - 12" 4 - 4⅛"	12 - 7½"r 30°	1 LH	17" x 36"

1 — Atlas supplies one 19"r 15° section with each switch
2 — Also sold by Aurora

PLAN 18 (AHM)

BRAND	STRAIGHT	CURVED	SWITCHES	SIZE
AHM	11 - 3¾"	12 - 7"r 30°	1 RH	17" x 31"
Atlas	10 - 5"	12 - 9¾"r 30°	1 RH	22" x 40"
Minitrix1	3 - 12" 1 - 4⅛"	12 - 7½"r 30°	1 RH	16" x 32"

1 — Also sold by Aurora

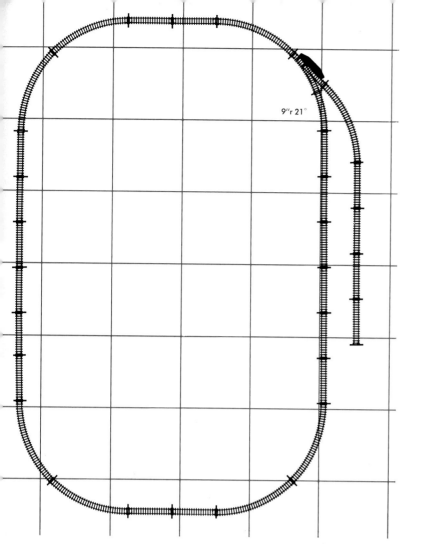

9″r 21°

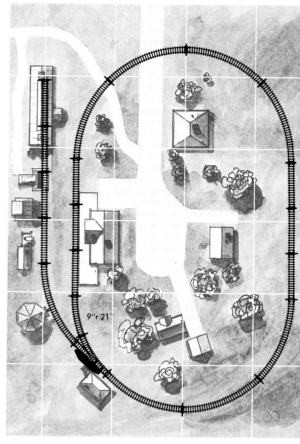

9″r 21°

PLAN 19 (AHM)

BRAND	STRAIGHT	CURVED	SWITCHES	SIZE
AHM	20 - 3¾″	9 - 9″r 45° 1 - 9″r 21°	1 RH	30″ x 42″
Minitrix[1]	4 - 12″ 8 - 4⅛″	13 - 7½″r 30°	1 RH	28″ x 40″

[1] — Also sold by Aurora

PLAN 20 (AHM)

BRAND	STRAIGHT	CURVED	SWITCHES	SIZE
AHM	10 - 3¾″	8 - 9″r 45° 1 - 9″r 21°	1 RH	23″ x 31″

PLAN 21 (Atlas)

BRAND	STRAIGHT	CURVED	SWITCHES	SIZE
Atlas	11 - 5″	15 - 9¾″r 30° 1 - 19″r 15°[1]	1 RH	30″ x 38″

[1] — Atlas supplies one 19″r 15° piece with each switch.

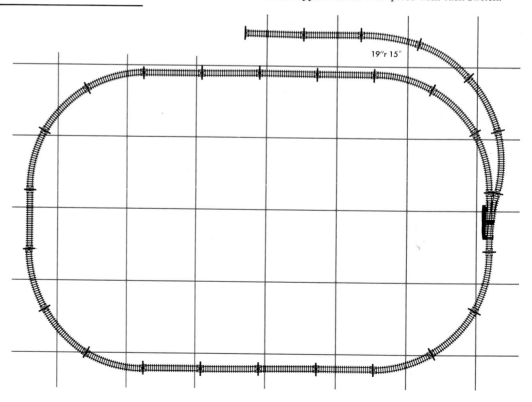

19″r 15°

Railroads with two switches

WITH two switches the operating possibilities of your railroad are greatly increased. With a pair of switches you can create alternate routes. Another way to obtain even more operating variety is to create dead-end spurs and sidetracks. You can add these dead ends to improve any track plan, not just these. What's more, you can add these spurs almost anywhere along your main line and you can change them around for variety. In general, it's better to use more than half of your switches to create spurs and only a few switches to make extra routes.

You can use switches to create spurs one way today and then you can combine them for new routes and other ideas next week.

A plan like 24 provides some operating variety. You can back cars into one siding but you have to push them into the other.

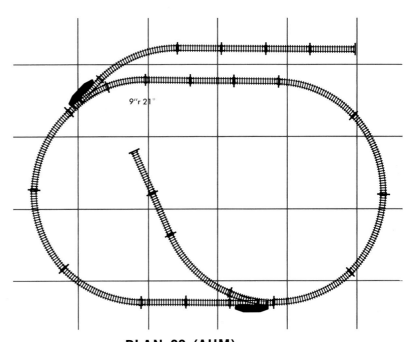

PLAN 22 (AHM)

BRAND	STRAIGHT	CURVED	SWITCHES	SIZE
AHM	11 - 3¾″	9 - 9″r 45° 1 - 9″r 21°	2 RH	23″ x 31″

PLAN 23 (Arnold Rapido)

BRAND	STRAIGHT	CURVED	SWITCHES	SIZE
Arnold Rapido[1]	8 - 9″	8 - 8″r 45° 2 - 17″r 15°	1 RH 1 LH	26″ x 44″

[1] — Also sold by Revell

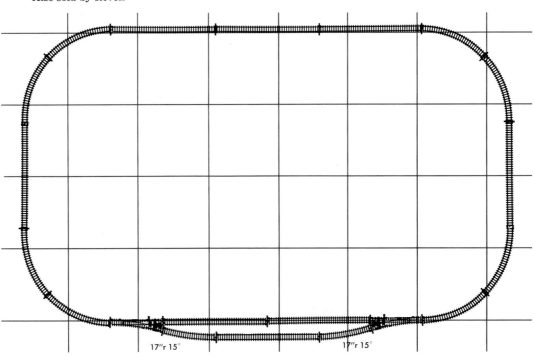

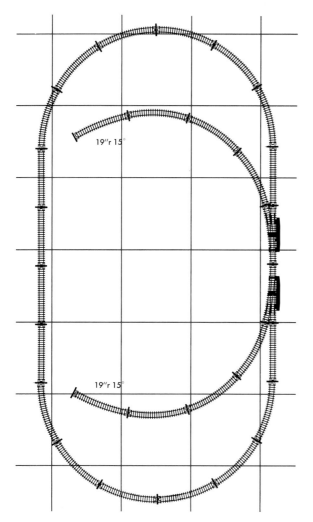

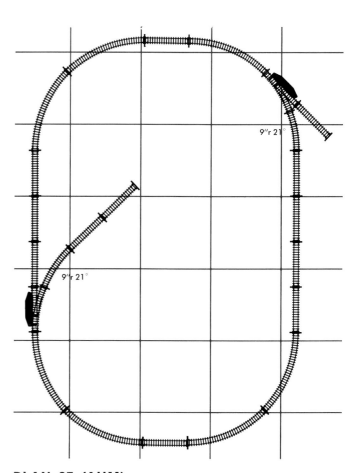

PLAN 24 (Atlas)

BRAND	STRAIGHT	CURVED	SWITCHES	SIZE
Atlas	6-5″	18 - 9¾″r 30°	1 RH, 1 LH	22″ x 40″
		2 - 19″r 15°		

[1] — Atlas supplies one 19″r 15° piece with each switch

PLAN 25 (AHM)

BRAND	STRAIGHT	CURVED	SWITCHES	SIZE
AHM	12 - 3¾″	7 - 9″r 45°	2 RH	32″ x 36″
		2 - 9″r 21°		

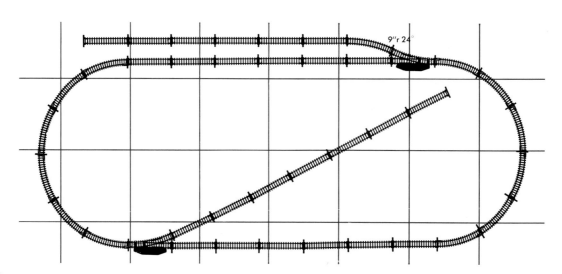

PLAN 26 (AHM)

BRAND	STRAIGHT	CURVED	SWITCHES	SIZE
AHM	25 - 3¾″	12 - 7″r 30°	1 RH, 1 LH	18″ x 42″
		1 - 9″r 24°		
Arnold Rapido[1]	8 - 9″	8 - 8″r 45°	1 RH, 1 LH	18″ x 38″
		2 17″r 15°		
Atlas	19 - 5″	12 - 9¾″r 30°	1 RH, 1 LH	24″ x 50″
		2 - 19″r 15°[2]		
Minitrix[3]	4 - 12″	13 - 7½″r 30°	1 RH, 1 LH	19″ x 36″
	5 - 4⅛″			

[1] — Also sold by Revell
[2] — Atlas supplies one 19″r 15° piece with each switch
[3] — Also sold by Aurora

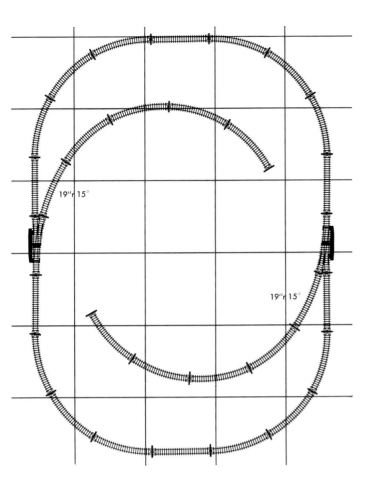

19″ r 15°

19″ r 15°

Many of the plans in this book were designed with the idea of getting as much track in a given area as possible. For this reason some plans include small-radius curves and some have S curves. However, you will find small-radius curves difficult to negotiate without a derailment if you operate long-wheelbase rolling stock such as 80-foot passenger cars or steam locomotives with six or more driving wheels. If you plan to operate this type of equipment, and you have the additional space, revise your plan by using proportionally larger-radius curved track. This will require a little more table area.

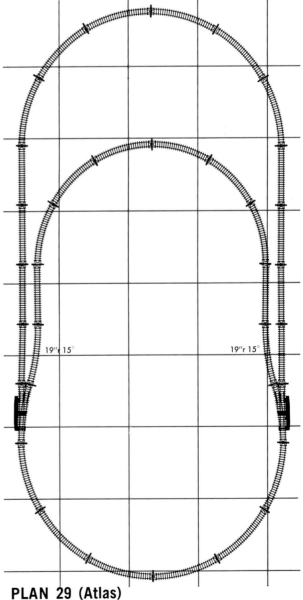

19″ r 15°

19″ r 15°

PLAN 27 (Atlas)

BRAND	STRAIGHT	CURVED	SWITCHES	SIZE
AHM	4 - 3¾″	20 - 7″r 30°	2 RH	21″ x 28″
Atlas	6 - 5″	20 - 9¾″r 30°	2 RH	27″ x 36″
		2 - 19″r 15°		
Minitrix[1]	6 - 4⅛″	20 - 7½″r 30°	2 RH	21″ x 28″

[1] — Also sold by Aurora

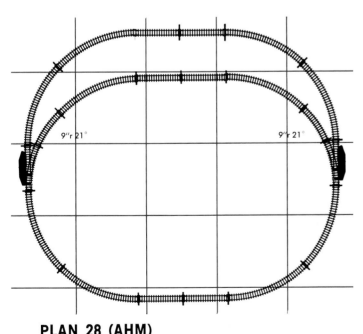

9″ r 21°

9″ r 21°

PLAN 28 (AHM)

BRAND	STRAIGHT	CURVED	SWITCHES	SIZE
AHM	6 - 3¾″	10 - 9″r 45°	1 RH, 1 LH	23″ x 28″
		2 - 9″r 21°		

PLAN 29 (Atlas)

BRAND	STRAIGHT	CURVED	SWITCHES	SIZE
Atlas	10 - 5″	12 - 11″r 30°	1 RH, 1 LH	24″ x 48″
		6 - 9¾″r 30°		
		2 - 19″r 15°[1]		

[1] —Atlas supplies one 19″r 15° piece with each switch

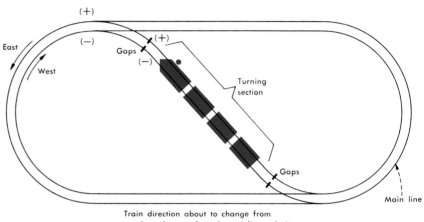

Westbound train

Train direction about to change from
westbound to eastbound. Mainline polarity
has been reversed.

Reverse-loop wiring*

You will notice that some plans have an M and an R marked near the track. These plans contain "turning track," which requires some special wiring. A turning track exists wherever you are able to get a train turned end for end. If we use the convention of calling clockwise movement westbound, then we can say we have a turning track wherever we can change a train from heading westbound to eastbound and vice versa.

Wherever there is a turning track we must create an isolated turning section and add a double-pole, double-throw electrical switch. These additions are necessary because to operate a locomotive in the forward direction the polarity of the track voltage must be positive on the right (engineer's) side. When the locomotive travels around a loop and re-enters the main line going in the opposite direction, the polarity of the mainline track voltage must be reversed if the locomotive is to continue going forward.

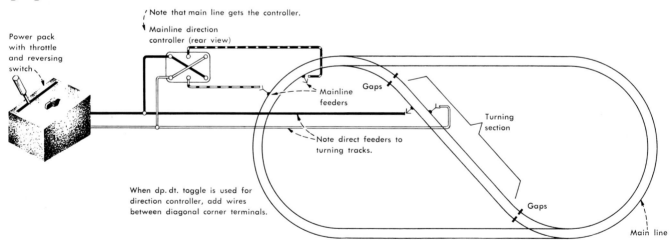

By providing one extra direction controller, mainline polarity can be changed
smoothly from westbound to eastbound while train is within the turning section.
If turning section is long enough, this can be done easily without stopping the
train and without jerking. The reversing switch on the power pack is still needed
for back-up moves on either main line or return track.

Heavy black lines mark the points where the main line and the turning section should be insulated from one another. This can be done in several ways. Some manufacturers sell insulated rail joiners for this purpose, while others sell special track sections called gap sections. If your track is already laid before you discover you have a turning track, you can cut gaps in the rails using a razor saw. Clean any metal chips

* This subject and many others are covered in detail in Linn Westcott's book How to Wire Your Model Railroad.

from the saw cut and then squirt a little Ambroid cement into the gap so it cannot close when the rail expands in hot weather.

Once you have the turning track isolated from the main track, the wiring is easy. You simply connect the turning section (marked R on plan) to the power pack terminals. The main line is connected to the power pack

through a dp.dt. switch as shown in the diagram. This switch becomes the mainline direction controller.

When operating, you must throw the direction controller after the entire train is in the turning section. This reverses mainline voltage polarity so your train can continue in the opposite direction as it exits the section.

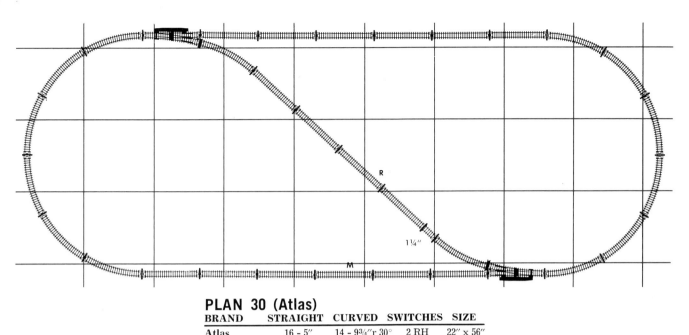

PLAN 30 (Atlas)

BRAND	STRAIGHT	CURVED	SWITCHES	SIZE
Atlas	16 - 5″ 1 - 1¼″	14 - 9¾″r 30°	2 RH	22″ x 56″

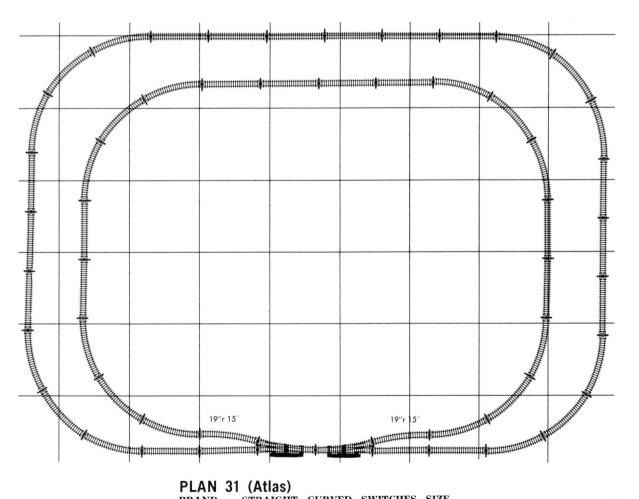

PLAN 31 (Atlas)

BRAND	STRAIGHT	CURVED	SWITCHES	SIZE
Atlas	24 - 5″	24 - 9¾″r 30° 2 - 19″r 15°[1]	1 RH, 1 LH	36″ x 50″

[1] — Atlas supplies one 19″r 15° piece with each switch

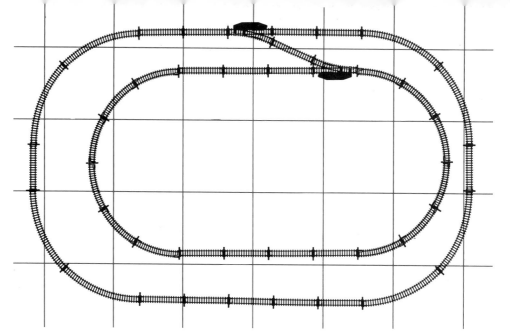

PLAN 32 (AHM)

BRAND	STRAIGHT	CURVED	SWITCHES	SIZE
AHM	19 - 3¾″	8 - 9″r 45°	2 RH	24″ x 38″
		12 - 7″r 30°		

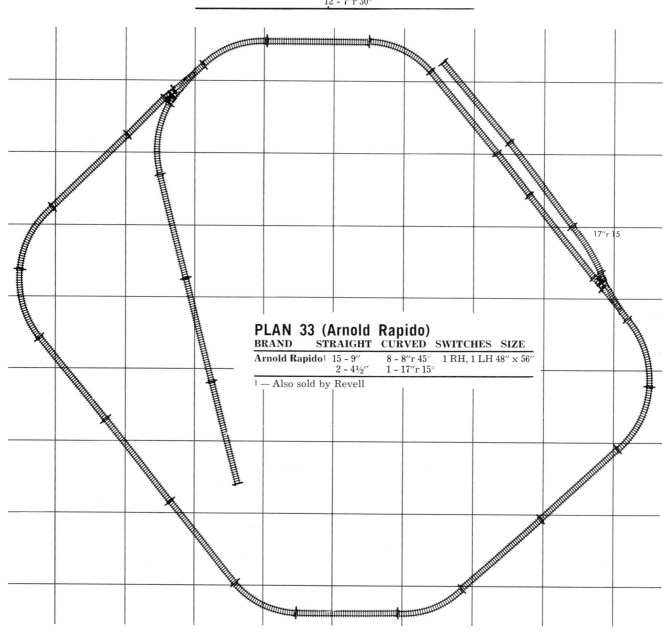

17″r 15

PLAN 33 (Arnold Rapido)

BRAND	STRAIGHT	CURVED	SWITCHES	SIZE
Arnold Rapido[1]	15 - 9″	8 - 8″r 45°	1 RH, 1 LH	48″ x 56″
	2 - 4½″	1 - 17″r 15°		

[1] — Also sold by Revell

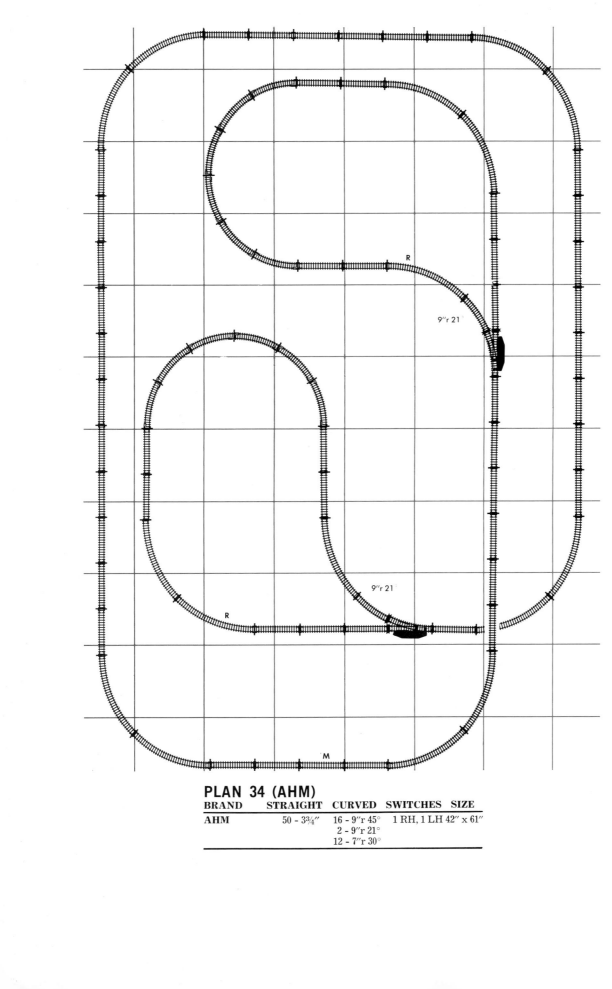

PLAN 34 (AHM)

BRAND	STRAIGHT	CURVED	SWITCHES	SIZE
AHM	50 - 3¾″	16 - 9″r 45°	1 RH, 1 LH	42″ x 61″
		2 - 9″r 21°		
		12 - 7″r 30°		

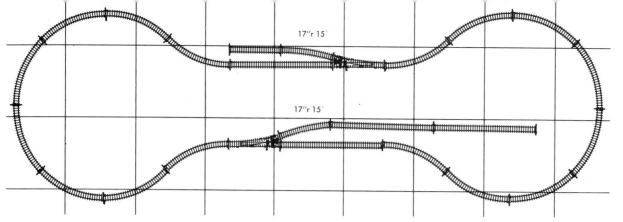

17"r 15°

17"r 15°

PLAN 35 (Arnold Rapido)

BRAND	STRAIGHT	CURVED	SWITCHES	SIZE
AHM	9 - 3¾"	20 - 7"r 30°	1 RH, 1 LH	16" x 42"
		2 - 9"r 24°		
Arnold Rapido[1]	- 9"	16 - 8"r 45°	1 RH, 1 LH	16" x 52"
	1 - 4½"	2 - 17"r 15°		
Atlas	9 - 5"	20 - 9¾"r 30°	1 RH, 1 LH	22" x 55"
		2 - 19"r 15°[2]		
Minitrix[3]	8 - 4⅛"	22 - 7½"r 30°	1 RH, 1 LH	16" x 50"

[1] — Also sold by Revell

[2] — Atlas supplies one 19"r 15° piece with each switch

[3] — Also sold by Aurora

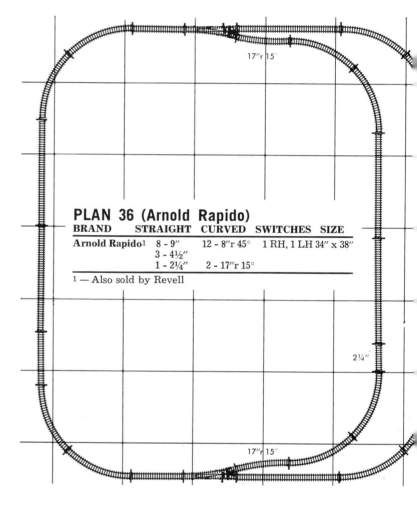

17"r 15°

2¼"

17"r 15°

PLAN 36 (Arnold Rapido)

BRAND	STRAIGHT	CURVED	SWITCHES	SIZE
Arnold Rapido[1]	8 - 9"	12 - 8"r 45°	1 RH, 1 LH	34" x 38"
	3 - 4½"			
	1 - 2¼"	2 - 17"r 15°		

[1] — Also sold by Revell

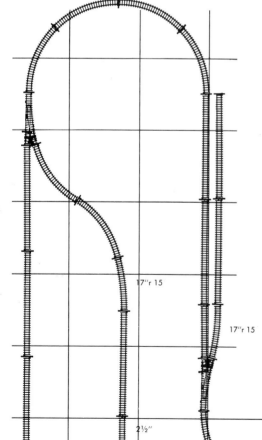

17"r 15

17"r 15

2½"

PLAN 37 (Arnold Rapido)

BRAND	STRAIGHT	CURVED	SWITCHES	SIZE
Arnold Rapido[1]	15 - 9"	19 - 8"r 45°	1 RH, 1 LH	48" x 52"
	4 - 4½"	2 - 8"r 15°		
	1 - 2¼"	2 - 17"r 15°		

[1] — Also sold by Revell

8"r 15°

8"r 15°

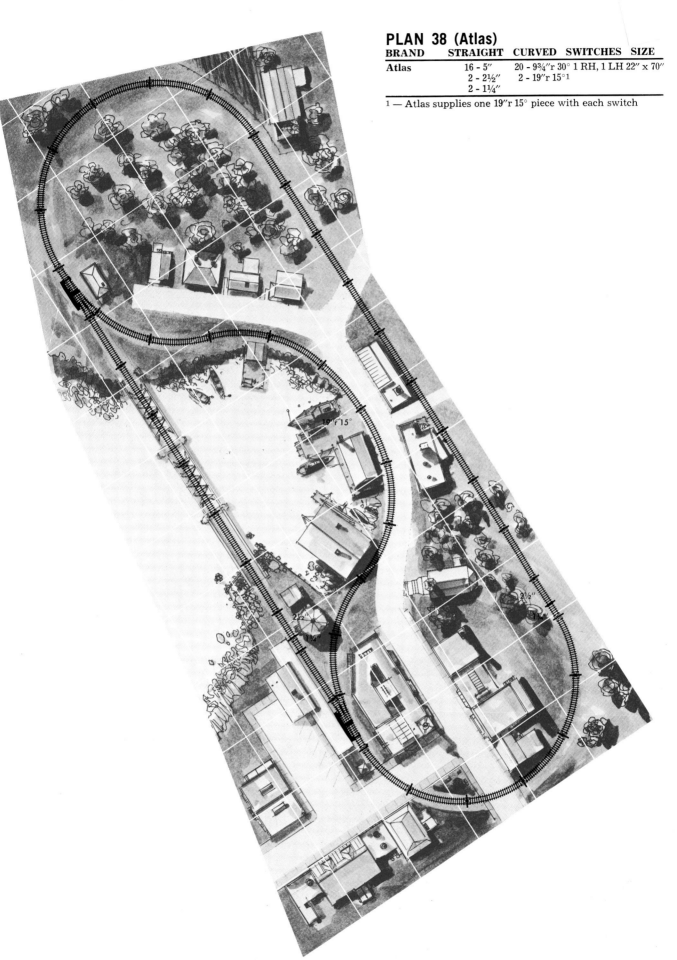

PLAN 38 (Atlas)

BRAND	STRAIGHT	CURVED	SWITCHES	SIZE
Atlas	16 – 5″	20 – 9¾″r 30°	1 RH, 1 LH	22″ x 70″
	2 – 2½″	2 – 19″r 15°1		
	2 – 1¼″			

1 — Atlas supplies one 19″r 15° piece with each switch

Railroads with three and four switches

THESE plans use switches to create two or more spurs for factories, enginehouses, freight loading, mines, quarries, and the like. This gives you lots of fun with switching operations. Some of the plans have a double-ended siding or "passing track." This helps the engine to get around some of the cars while switching. You can also use the siding to store one train while another is running. If you want two trains to run at the same time, you must run them in the same direction on these plans. To run trains in opposite directions you need more than one passing track or else a double-track line. Some plans in this book have these two-train provisions.

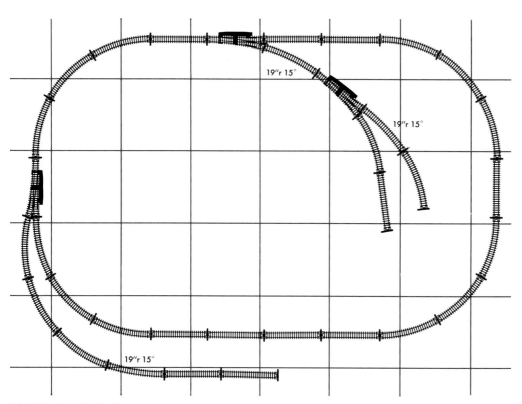

19"r 15°

19"r 15°

19"r 15°

PLAN 39 (Atlas)

BRAND	STRAIGHT	CURVED	SWITCHES	SIZE
Atlas	11 - 5"	17 - 9¾"r 30°	3 RH	30" x 38"
		3 - 19"r 15°1		

1 — Atlas supplies one 19"r 15° piece with each switch

PLAN 40 (AHM)

BRAND	STRAIGHT	CURVED	SWITCHES	SIZE
AHM	27 - 3¾"	1 - 9"r 45°	2 RH, 1 LH	17" x 54"
		2 - 9"r 24°		
		1 - 9"r 21°		
		12 - 7"r 30°		

9"r 24°

9"r 21°

9"r 24°

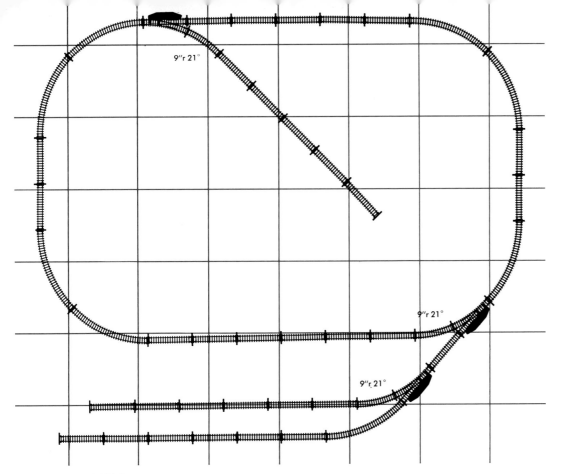

PLAN 41 (AHM)

BRAND	STRAIGHT	CURVED	SWITCHES	SIZE
AHM	33 - 3¾″	8 - 9″r 45° 3 - 9″r 21°	3 RH	36″ x 42″
Minitrix[1]	7 - 12″ 6 - 4⅛″	14 - 7½″r 30°	3 RH	36″ x 44″

[1] — Also sold by Aurora

PLAN 42 (AHM)

BRAND	STRAIGHT	CURVED	SWITCHES	SIZE
AHM	25 - 3¾″	9 - 9″r 45° 2 - 9″r 21°	3 RH	30″ x 42″
Minitrix[1]	6 - 12″ 7 - 4⅛″	14 - 7½″r 30°	3 RH	28″ x 40″

[1] — Also sold by Aurora

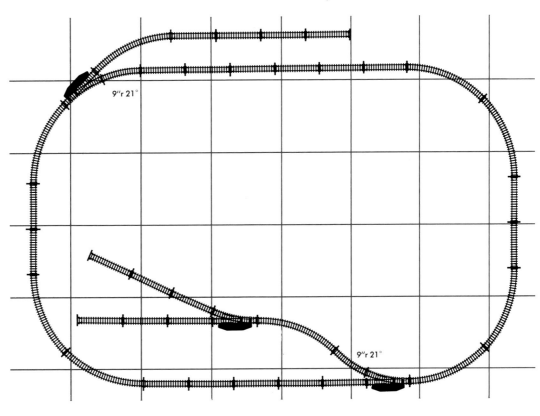

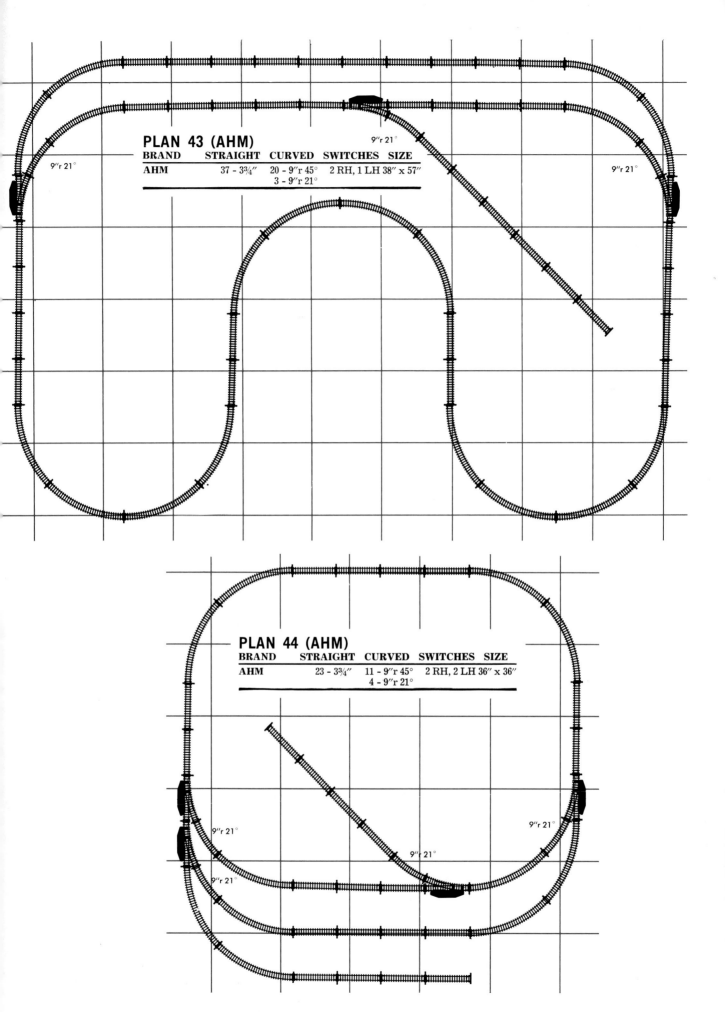

PLAN 43 (AHM)

BRAND	STRAIGHT	CURVED	SWITCHES	SIZE
AHM	37 - 3¾"	20 - 9"r 45°	2 RH, 1 LH	38" x 57"
		3 - 9"r 21°		

9"r 21°
9"r 21°
9"r 21°
9"r 21°

PLAN 44 (AHM)

BRAND	STRAIGHT	CURVED	SWITCHES	SIZE
AHM	23 - 3¾"	11 - 9"r 45°	2 RH, 2 LH	36" x 36"
		4 - 9"r 21°		

9"r 21°
9"r 21°
9"r 21°
9"r 21°

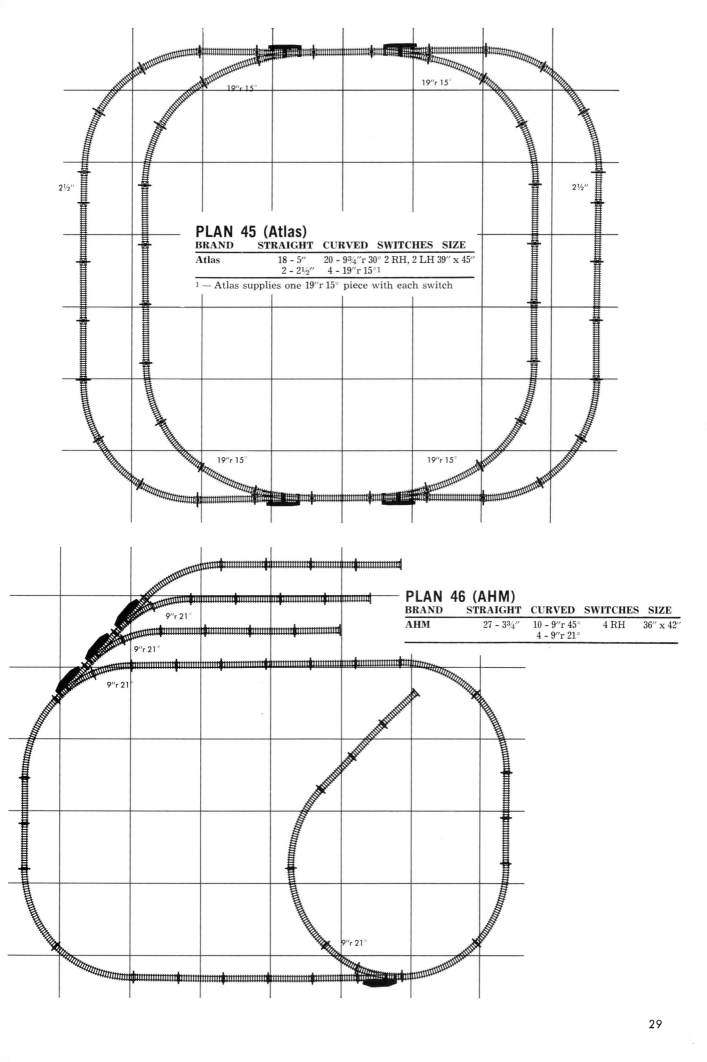

PLAN 45 (Atlas)

BRAND	STRAIGHT	CURVED	SWITCHES	SIZE
Atlas	18 - 5″ 2 - 2½″	20 - 9¾″r 30° 4 - 19″r 15°[1]	2 RH, 2 LH	39″ x 45″

[1] — Atlas supplies one 19″r 15° piece with each switch

19″r 15°

19″r 15°

2½″

2½″

19″r 15°

19″r 15°

PLAN 46 (AHM)

BRAND	STRAIGHT	CURVED	SWITCHES	SIZE
AHM	27 - 3¾″	10 - 9″r 45° 4 - 9″r 21°	4 RH	36″ x 42″

9″r 21°

9″r 21°

9″r 21°

9″r 21°

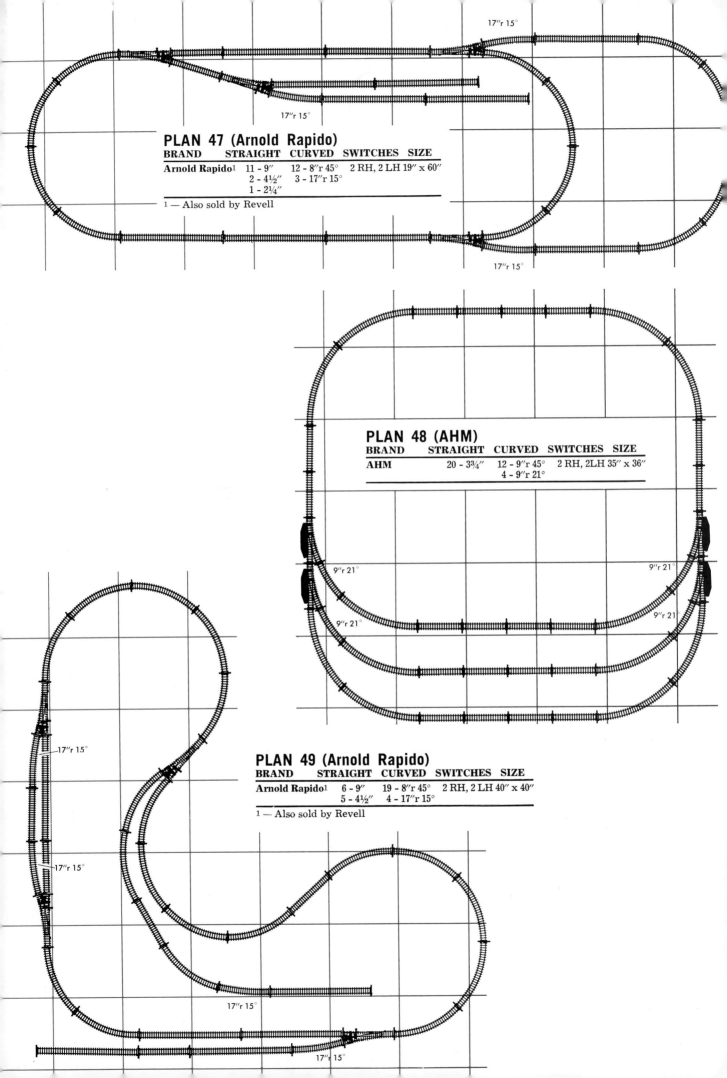

PLAN 47 (Arnold Rapido)

BRAND	STRAIGHT	CURVED	SWITCHES	SIZE
Arnold Rapido[1]	11 - 9″	12 - 8″r 45°	2 RH, 2 LH	19″ x 60″
	2 - 4½″	3 - 17″r 15°		
	1 - 2¼″			

[1] — Also sold by Revell

17″r 15°

17″r 15°

17″r 15°

PLAN 48 (AHM)

BRAND	STRAIGHT	CURVED	SWITCHES	SIZE
AHM	20 - 3¾″	12 - 9″r 45°	2 RH, 2LH	35″ x 36″
		4 - 9″r 21°		

9″r 21°

9″r 21°

9″r 21°

9″r 21

PLAN 49 (Arnold Rapido)

BRAND	STRAIGHT	CURVED	SWITCHES	SIZE
Arnold Rapido[1]	6 - 9″	19 - 8″r 45°	2 RH, 2 LH	40″ x 40″
	5 - 4½″	4 - 17″r 15°		

[1] — Also sold by Revell

17″r 15°

17″r 15°

17″r 15°

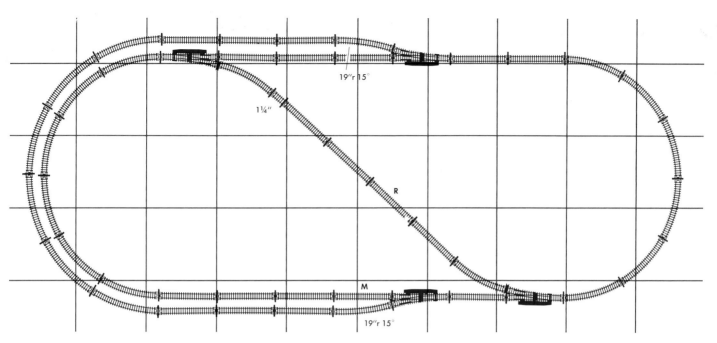

PLAN 50 (Atlas)

BRAND	STRAIGHT	CURVED	SWITCHES	SIZE
Atlas	20 - 5″	14 - 9¾″r 30°	3 RH, 1 LH	24″ x 56″
	1 - 1¼″	6 - 11″r 30°		
		2 - 19″r 15°[1]		

[1] — Atlas supplies one 19″r 15° piece with each switch

PLAN 51 (Atlas)

BRAND	STRAIGHT	CURVED	SWITCHES	SIZE
Atlas	20 - 5″	12 - 11″r 30°	2 RH, 2 LH	38″ x 54″
	2 - 1¼″	10 - 9¾″r 30°		
		10 - 19″r 30°[1]		
		10 - 19″r 15°[1]		

[1] — Atlas supplies one 19″r 15° piece with each switch

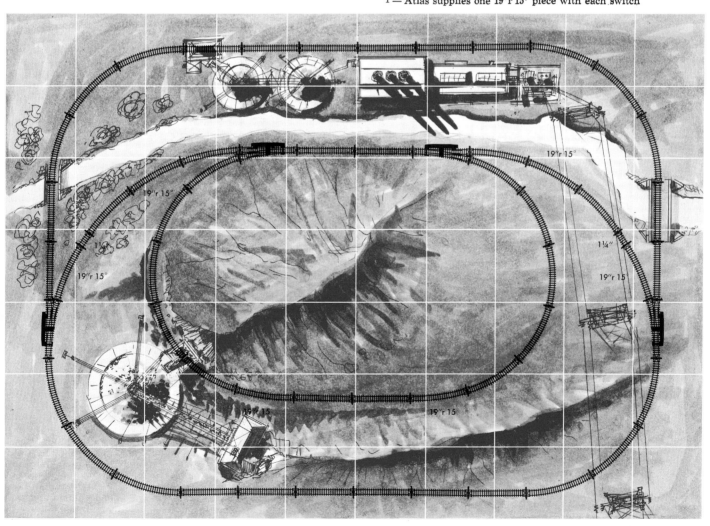

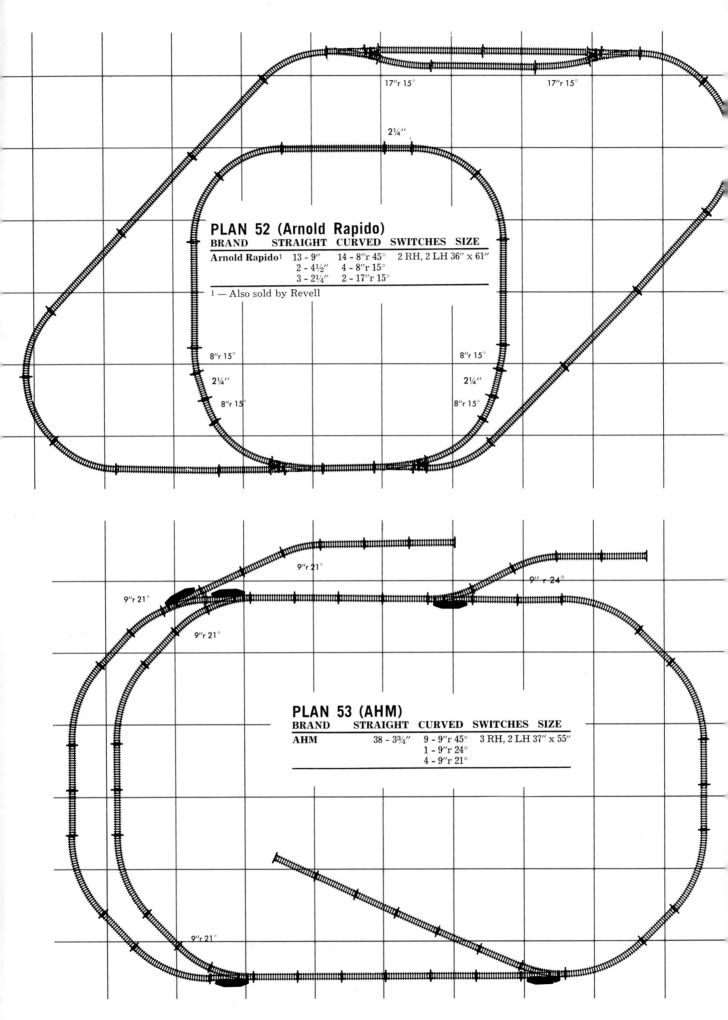

17"r 15°   17"r 15°

2¼"

PLAN 52 (Arnold Rapido)

BRAND	STRAIGHT	CURVED	SWITCHES	SIZE
Arnold Rapido[1]	13 - 9"	14 - 8"r 45°	2 RH, 2 LH	36" x 61"
	2 - 4½"	4 - 8"r 15°		
	3 - 2¼"	2 - 17"r 15°		

[1] — Also sold by Revell

8"r 15°   8"r 15°

2¼"   2¼"

8"r 15°   8"r 15°

9"r 21°   9"r 24°

9"r 21°

9"r 21°

PLAN 53 (AHM)

BRAND	STRAIGHT	CURVED	SWITCHES	SIZE
AHM	38 - 3¾"	9 - 9"r 45°	3 RH, 2 LH	37" x 55"
		1 - 9"r 24°		
		4 - 9"r 21°		

9"r 21°

Large railroads

AS you purchase more track and additional switches, the railroad possibilities become almost infinite. You'll probably build your railroad a little differently here and there, but these plans will give you ideas to start with.

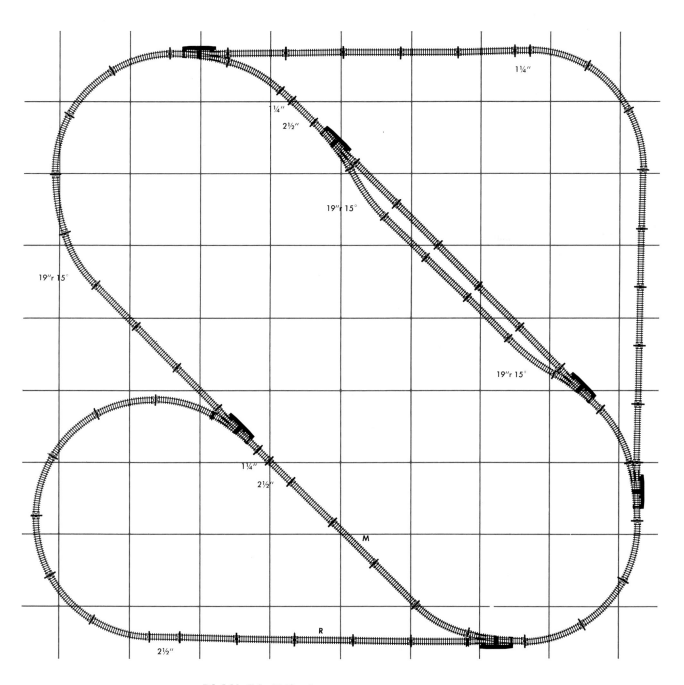

PLAN 54 (Atlas)

BRAND	STRAIGHT	CURVED	SWITCHES	SIZE
Atlas	29 - 5″	20 - 9¾″r 30°	3 RH, 2 LH	50″ x 52″
	3 - 2½″	3 - 19″r 15° 1		
	3 - 1¼″			

1 — Atlas supplies one 19″r 15° piece with each switch

PLAN 56 (Atlas)

BRAND	STRAIGHT	CURVED	SWITCHES	SIZE
Atlas	30 - 5"	12 - 11"r 30°	2 RH, 4 LH	56" x 5
	3 - 2½"	8 - 9¾"r 30°		
	3 - 1¼"	14 - 19"r 15°[1]		

[1] — Atlas supplies one 19"r 15° piece with each switch

PLAN 55 (Atlas)

BRAND	STRAIGHT	CURVED	SWITCHES	SIZE
Atlas	33 - 5"	21 - 9¾"r 30°	3 RH, 2 LH	45" x 56"
	2 - 2½"	5 - 19"r 15° [1]		

[1] — Atlas supplies one 19"r 15° piece with each switch

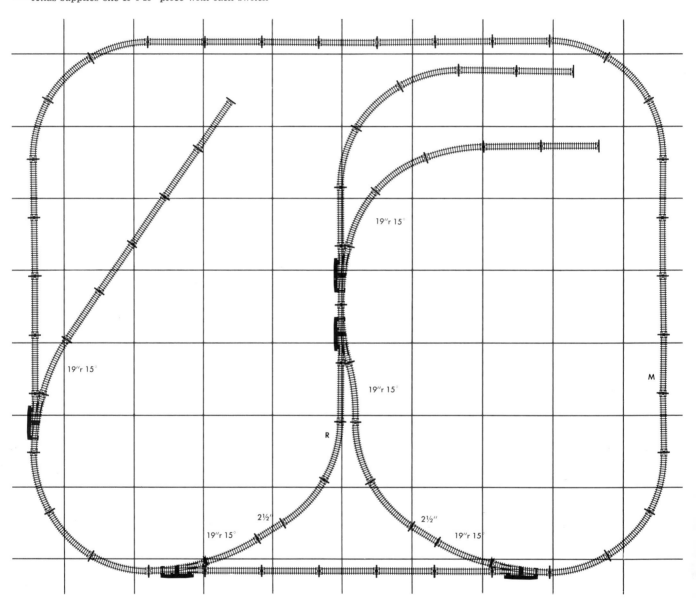

19"r 15°

19"r 15°

19"r 15°

19"r 15°

M

R

2½"

2½"

19"r 15°

19"r 15°

PLAN 57

BRAND	STRAIGHT	CURVED	SWITCHES	SIZE
Arnold Rapido[1]	20 - 9"	17 - 8"r 45°	2 RH, 2 LH	35" x 6
	5 - 4½"	4 - 17"r 15°		
	2 - 2¼"			

[1] — Also sold by Revell

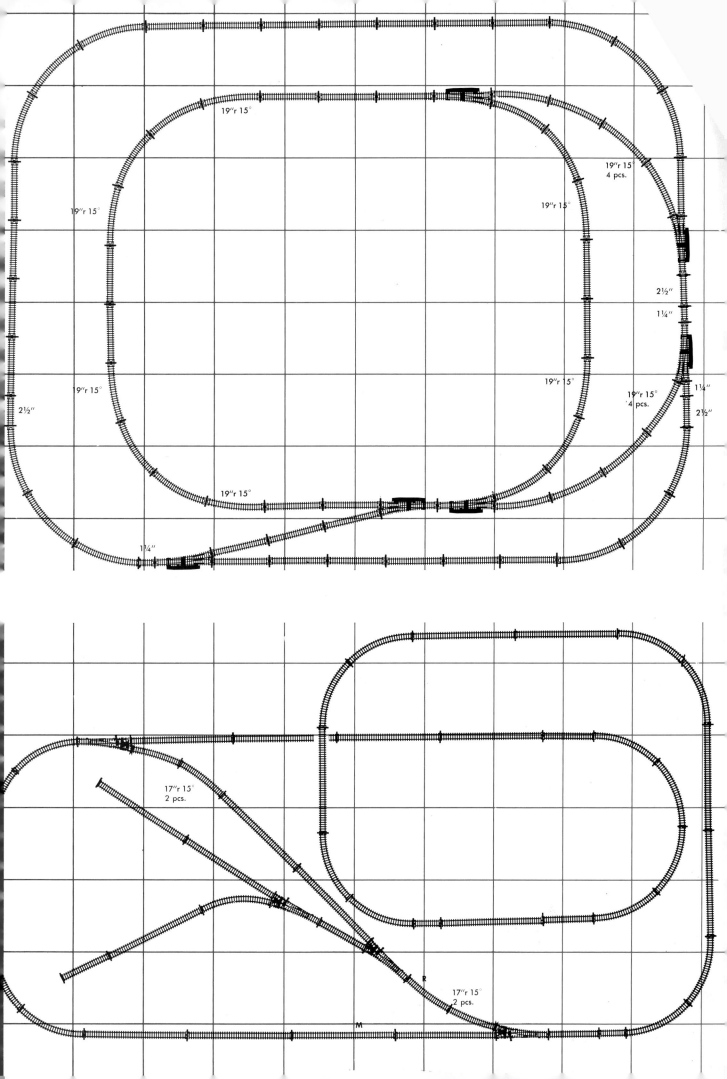

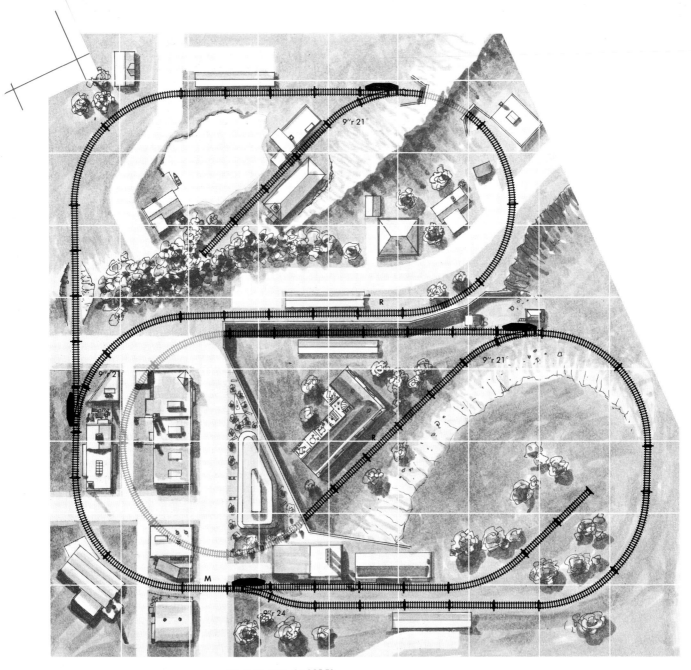

PLAN 58 (AHM)

BRAND	STRAIGHT	CURVED	SWITCHES	SIZE
AHM	42 - 3¾″	19 - 9″r 45°	2 RH, 2 LH	44″ x 50″
		1 - 9″r 24°		
		3 - 9″r 21°		

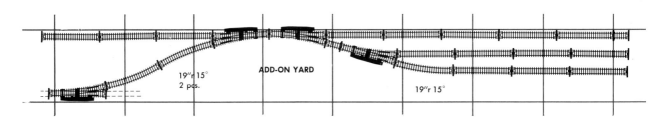

ADD-ON YARD

19″r 15°
2 pcs.

19″r 15°

PLAN 59 (Atlas)

BRAND	STRAIGHT	CURVED	SWITCHES	SIZE
Atlas	15 - 5″	3 - 19″r 15°[1]	1 RH, 3 LH	6″ x 52″
	2 - 1¼″			

[1] — Atlas supplies one 19″r 15° piece with each switch

Permanent railroads

THE remaining plans in this book are the type you will probably choose for a permanent railroad. While we've called these "permanent railroads," we hope you will feel free to revise and rebuild any part of them at any time. It's just that these layouts are likely to remain the same for a longer time than the geometric plans which are shown on preceding pages.

A permanent layout needs buildings and scenery. You could think of it as a miniature world with a railroad running through it. These plans include scenery suggestions — but feel free to try an arrangement of your own.

When planning scenery, try to keep reasonably close to scale dimensions where possible. You can calculate N scale dimensions by dividing the prototype dimensions by 160. For instance, the typical width of a two-lane highway is about 20 feet. The width of an N scale highway can be calculated by dividing 20 feet by 160, which equals approximately 1½". At the hobby shop you can buy an N scale rule. It will enable you to measure directly in scale feet, thereby eliminating all the calculations.

One area where scale authenticity has to be compromised is in the construction of mountains. Even a small 6000-foot mountain would be close to 40 feet high in N scale. You have to represent it with something much smaller, like 40" or even less. The lines across the plans represent 6" squares. If you draw these on the mounting surface it will help you locate various features.

The time setting of the layout is important to serious modelers. Choose the period of railroading that you like best. Try to be consistent. Diesel locomotives, for example, would certainly be out of place on a turn-of-the-century layout.

As you get more involved in the hobby of model railroading you'll find there is much more to it than laying track and operating the trains, although these are certainly fun. The hobby can overlap into the fields of railroad history, architecture, geography, electronics, mechanical engineering, and many others. There is enough creative challenge in model railroading for it to become a lifetime hobby.

In building these railroads, we suggest that you read the copy beside every plan, not just that with the one you will build.

Two-Train operation*

To operate two trains simultaneously under separate control, you must divide the track into sections which are electrically insulated from one another. This can be done in several ways. Some manufacturers sell insulated rail joiners for this purpose, while others sell special

---

* This subject and many others are covered in detail in Linn Westcott's book HOW TO WIRE YOUR MODEL RAILROAD.

track sections. If your track is already laid before you decide you want two-train operation, you can cut gaps in the rails using a razor saw. Saw all the way through the rail. Then clean any metal chips from the saw cut. Squirt a little Ambroid cement into the gap so it cannot close if the rail expands in hot weather.

You then connect electrical feeder wires from each insulated section (called a block) to the center terminals of a dp.dt. switch. The outputs of two power packs are connected to the switch terminals as illustrated. When connected as shown, throwing switch 1 to the right connects power pack A, on the right, to block 1. Throwing switch 1 to the left connects power pack B, on the left, to block 1. You will need as many dp.dt. switches as you have blocks.

Normally the switches are mounted on a control panel containing a schematic of the track plan. Switches are located on the schematic in locations corresponding to the blocks they control. The control panel shown was built for one of our model railroads.

A power pack is placed at each side of the control panel and you throw the switches in your direction as your train proceeds around the layout. As your train leaves a block you return the switch for that block to the OFF position so the other "engineer" knows the block is now unoccupied.

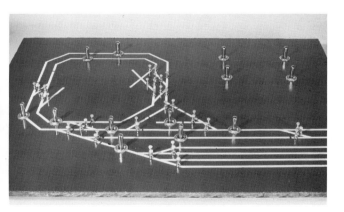

This control panel was built for the N scale New York & Quebec RR. which was the 1969 project railroad featured in **MODEL RAILROADER** magazine.

Throwing switch 1 to the right connects power pack A, on the right, to block 1. Throwing it to the left connects power pack B, on the left, to block 1.

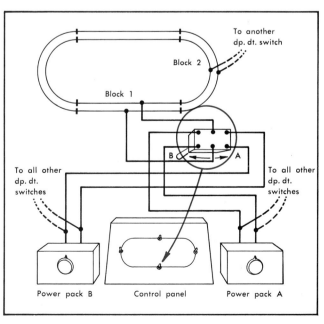

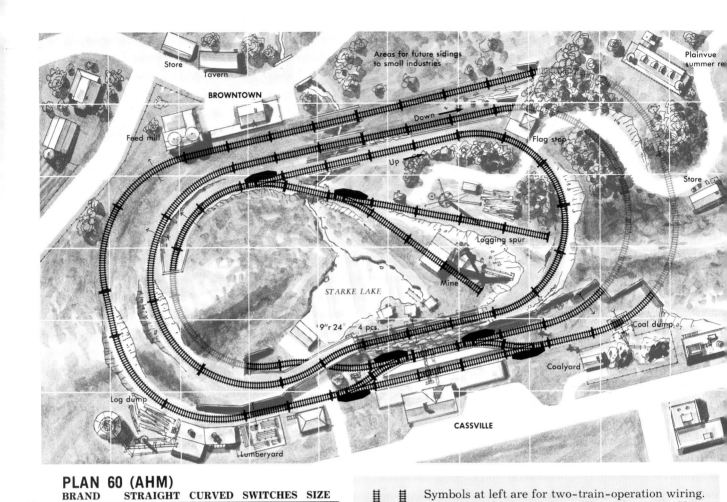

PLAN 60 (AHM)

BRAND	STRAIGHT	CURVED	SWITCHES	SIZE
AHM	39 - 3¾"	16 - 9"r 45°	4 RH, 2 LH	24" x 50"
		4 - 9"r 24°		
		12 - 7"r 30°		

Symbols at left are for two-train-operation wiring. Far left symbol — gaps or insulated joiners. Near left symbol — electrical feeder wire connections.

The Dapperling RR.

Choosing a name for your permanent railroad is part of the fun. Some model railroaders use names of real railroads or other serious names, while others dream up humorous or clever names. Some of these names sound ridiculous to all but the persons who thought them up.

For instance, a dapperling is a little fellow who is neat and trim in appearance. We've stretched the definition slightly to describe this layout.

You may also want to make up a little story describing the operation of your railroad.

The Dapperling RR. serves Cassville, Browntown, a mine, and a logging operation. During the summer, limited passenger service is provided between Cassville and the road leading to the Plainue Resort.

For helper version, use a bridge, raising track X-X.

CENNPEN RR.
(Helper District)

Helper districts are used in mountainous areas where additional motive power is needed to pull the trains up steep grades. This makes for an interesting operation. The helper engines are coupled on at Payola Station for the hard uphill pull around Muleshoe Curve to Presson. From here the trains can go it alone so the helpers are uncoupled. A train proceeds into the tunnel, where it is stopped while the helper backs around to Payola Station. The train then proceeds through the tunnel, repeating the route for as many times as you want until you decide to go up the mountain grade again.

You can build this layout on one level, using a crossing as shown. If you do this you will have to imagine the train is going uphill when you reach Payola Station. If you want more realism, you'll have to actually raise a good portion of the track. This will require an overpass instead of a crossing, as shown in the elevated version.

ELEVATED VERSION

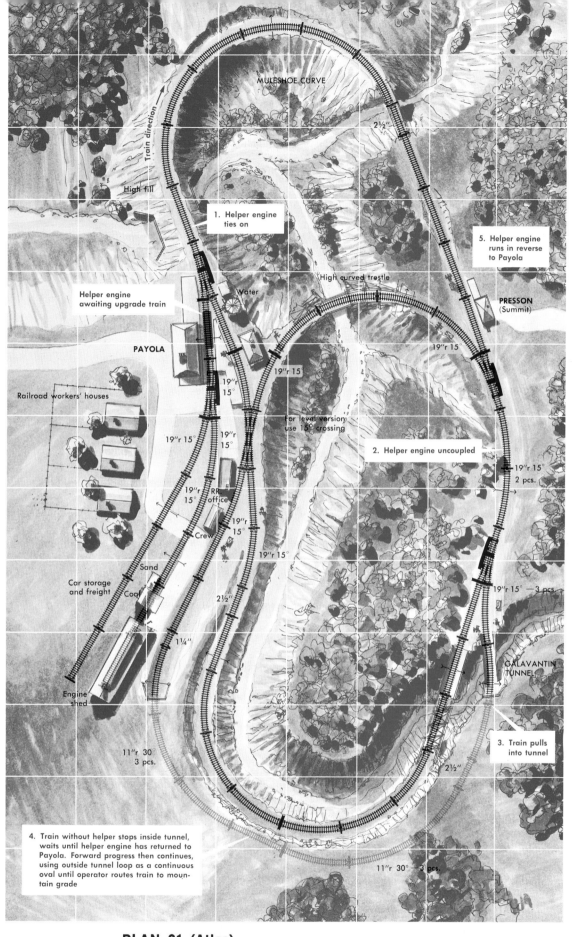

MULESHOE CURVE

Train direction

High fill

1. Helper engine ties on

2½"

5. Helper engine runs in reverse to Payola

Water

High curved trestle

Helper engine awaiting upgrade train

PRESSON (Summit)

PAYOLA

19"r 15°

19"r 15

19"r 15°

Railroad workers' houses

For level version use 15° crossing

2. Helper engine uncoupled

19"r 15° 2 pcs.

19"r 15°

19"r 15°

RR office

19"r 15°

Crew

19"r 15°

Sand

19"r 15°

Car storage and freight

Coal

19"r 15° — 3 pcs.

2½"

1¼"

GALAVANTIN TUNNEL

Engine shed

3. Train pulls into tunnel

11"r 30 3 pcs.

2½"

4. Train without helper stops inside tunnel, waits until helper engine has returned to Payola. Forward progress then continues, using outside tunnel loop as a continuous oval until operator routes train to mountain grade

11"r 30° — 3 pcs.

PLAN 61 (Atlas)

BRAND	STRAIGHT	CURVED	SWITCHES	CROSSING	SIZE
Atlas	22 – 5″	13 – 19″r 15°[1]	2 RH, 2 LH	1 – 15°	38″ x 70″
	3 – 2½″	6 – 11″r 30°			
	1 – 1¼″	15 – 9¾″r 30°			

[1] — Atlas supplies one 19″r 15° piece with each switch

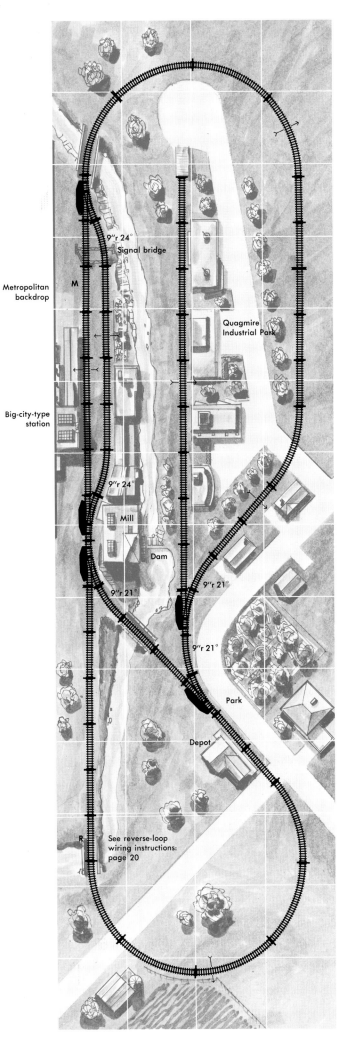

9"r 24°
Signal bridge

Metropolitan
backdrop

M

Quagmire
Industrial Park

Big-city-type
station

9"r 24°

Mill

Dam

9"r 21°

9"r 21°

9"r 21°

Park

Depot

R

See reverse-loop
wiring instructions:
page 20

PLAN 62 (AHM)

BRAND	STRAIGHT	CURVED	SWITCHES	SIZE
AHM	36 - 3¾"	9 - 9"r 45°	3 RH, 2LH	20" x 76"
		2 - 9"r 24°		
		3 - 9"r 21°		

E, Z & KWICK RR.

This layout is truly easy and quick to construct. It is a good beginner's railroad. All track is on the same level and the scenery is easy to build.

The single long industrial spur can be used as a storage place for cars not in use. It can be expanded into a small yard when you begin to acquire more cars.

This plan contains a turning track which also adds to the operating variety. This requires some special wiring which is explained for plan 30.

WESTERN COPPERVILLE RR.

Ore from the Penny Copper strip-mining district is transported by the Western Copperville RR. to the foundries at Midvale. Copper ingots and some finished products are shipped from Midvale to the industrial centers of the Midwest. The Western Copperville RR. also runs passenger service on its double-track main line between Copperville and Midvale and points east.

On this layout you can run two trains in opposite directions, and for variety you can occasionally interchange them if you're careful.

You might want to use a very steep grade (say about 8 percent) for the branch line which serves the Penny Copper mining district. This would be acceptable because the cars would always be empty going uphill.

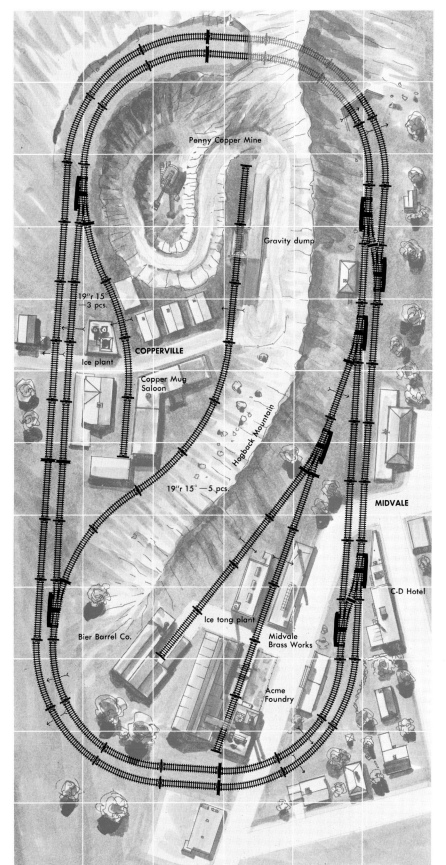

PLAN 63 (Atlas)

BRAND	STRAIGHT	CURVED	SWITCHES	SIZE
Atlas	43 - 5″	12 - 11″r 30°	5 RH, 3 LH	28″ x 62″
		12 - 9¾″r 30°		
		8 - 19″r 15°1		

1 — Atlas supplies one 19″r 15° piece with each switch

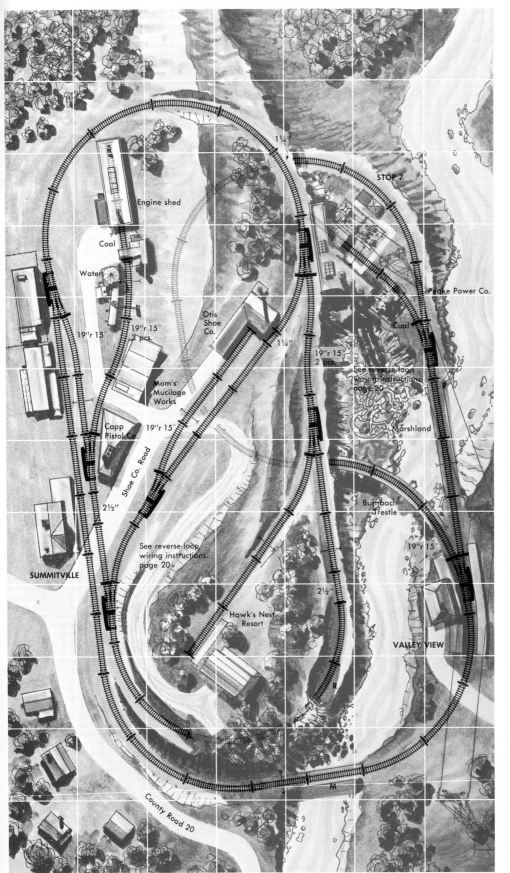

Engine shed

STOP 7

Coal

Water

Peake Power Co.

Otis
Shoe
Co.

Coal

1¼″

19″r 15°
3 pcs.

19″r 15°

19″r 15°
2 pcs.

See reverse-loop
wiring instructions:
page 20

Marshland

Mom's
Mucilage
Works

Capp
Pistol Co.

19″r 15°

Shoe Co. Road

Burnbach
Trestle

2½″

19″r 15°

See reverse-loop
wiring instructions:
page 20

SUMMITVILLE

2½″

Hawk's Nest
Resort

VALLEY VIEW

R

M

County Road 20

VALLEY VIEW & SUMMITVILLE RR.

This is a folded loop-to-loop plan. If you were to straighten it out you would have a long section of straight track with a return loop at each end. Even though the towns of Valley View and Summitville are physically very close to each other on the layout, they are at opposite ends of the track route. With a little imagination you can picture this as a railroad offering high-speed passenger service between the two cities. There is also seasonal passenger service to the popular Hawk's Nest Resort.

Two short passenger trains can be operated simultaneously on this layout; but it will take some concentration, because you have two reverse loops to worry about.

GREAT O RR.

Here is a layout which offers lots of operating variety. You can run both freight and passenger service simultaneously. Freight trains can be made up in the yard area while passenger trains run on the inner loop under Union Station. Freights can also run from the yard area to the factory district and around the outer loop under Union Station without disrupting passenger service.

Another feature of this layout is the large storage areas for both cars and locomotives.

PLAN 64 (Atlas)

BRAND	STRAIGHT	CURVED	SWITCHES	SIZE
Atlas	28 - 5″	12 - 11″r 30°	4 RH, 4 LH	33″ x 58″
	2 - 2½″	21 - 9¾″r 30°		
	2 - 1¼″	8 - 19″r 15°1		

1 — Atlas supplies one 19″r 15° piece with each switch

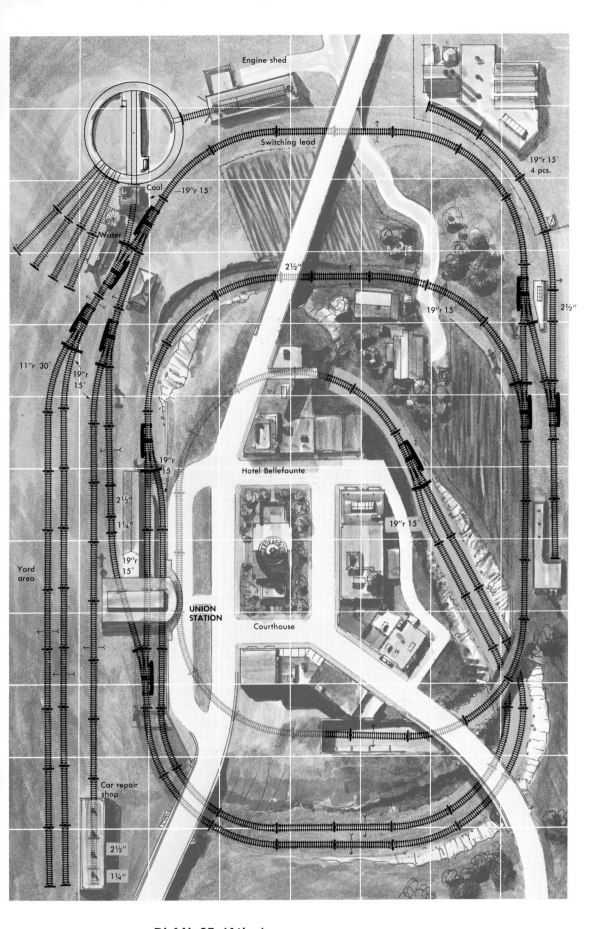

PLAN 65 (Atlas)

BRAND	STRAIGHT	CURVED	SWITCHES	SIZE
Atlas	67 – 5″	18 – 11″r 30°	1 RH, 9 LH	44″ x 65″
	4 – 2½″	18 – 9¾″r 30°		
	2 – 1¼″	11 – 19″r 15°[1]		

[1] — Atlas supplies one 19″r 15° piece with each switch